Nicholas Nickleby

Charles Dickens

Level 4

Retold by Chris Rice

Series Editors: Andy Hopkins and Jocelyn Potter

Pearson Education Limited
Edinburgh Gate, Harlow,
Essex CM20 2JE, England
and Associated Companies throughout the world.

Pack ISBN: 978-1-4058-5220-3
Book ISBN: 978-1-4058-5083-4
CD-ROM ISBN: 978-1-4058-5084-1

First edition published 2004
This edition published 2007

3 5 7 9 10 8 6 4 2

Text copyright © Penguin Books Ltd 2004
This edition copyright © Pearson Education Ltd 2007
Illustrations by Julián Totino Tedesco

Set in 11/13pt A. Garamond
Printed in China
SWTC/02

Produced for the Publishers by AC Estudio Editorial S.L.

Published by Pearson Education Ltd in association with Penguin Books Ltd,
both companies being subsidiaries of Pearson Plc.

Acknowledgements
We are grateful to the following for permission to reproduce photographs:

Getty Images: page 74 (4) (Hulton Archive); **Mary Evans Picture Library**: page 74 (1), (2), (3), (5);
The Charles Dickens Museum: page 74 (6) (Phiz) (Hoblot Knight Browne)

Picture Research by Hilary Luckcock

Every effort has been made to trace the copyright holders and we apologise in advance for any
unintentional omissions. We would be pleased to insert the appropriate acknowledgement
in any subsequent edition of this publication.

For a complete list of the titles available in the Penguin Active Reading series please write to your local
Pearson Longman office or to: Penguin Readers Marketing Department, Pearson Education,
Edinburgh Gate, Harlow, Essex CM20 2JE, England.

Contents

1.1 What's the book about?

Discuss these questions.

1 Look at the picture on the front cover and think about city life in the 1800s. How was life worse for: poor people? women? children?

2 What other books by Charles Dickens do you know? What qualities do they share?

3 Imagine these people are strangers at a party. Who would you talk to first? Who would you not talk to? Why?

1.2 What happens first?

Look at the pictures on pages 1–11. Do you think these statements are true (✓) or false (✗)?

1 ☐ Ralph Nickleby, the man in each of the first three pictures, is very popular.

2 ☐ Nicholas Nickleby and his family (page 4) are happy.

3 ☐ Nicholas (pages 8–9) goes on a long journey.

4 ☐ Smike (page 11) is afraid of Nicholas.

CHAPTER 1

Uncle Ralph

'I can understand a broken neck or a broken leg,
but not a broken heart.'

M r Ralph Nickleby closed the thick book that contained the names of all the people who **owe**d him money. His money-lending business was doing well, he thought with a satisfied smile. Life had never been better. It was true that he had never married, he had no friends and he was unpopular with his neighbours, but he did not care. People admired him because he was rich, and that was good enough for him. In his world, money was the only thing that mattered.

While Mr Nickleby was congratulating himself on his own success, there was a knock at the door. A tall, middle-aged man with strange, wild eyes walked into the room. It was Newman Noggs, Mr Nickleby's **clerk**.

owe /əʊ/ (v) to have to pay someone that you have borrowed money from
clerk /klɑːk/ (n) someone who works at a desk in an office

'What do you want, Newman?' Mr Nickleby said, annoyed by his interruption.

'I have a letter for you,' the clerk replied, one eye looking at his employer, the other looking out of the window.

'Well, bring it here, man!' Mr Nickleby said impatiently.

Newman took the letter carefully out of his badly fitting suit, carried it slowly across the room and gave it to his employer.

Mr Nickleby read it quickly. 'My brother's dead,' he said. 'That was sudden.' He stood up, walked across to the window, and stared thoughtfully through its dirty glass into the smoke-blackened **yard** behind his house.

'Children alive?' Noggs asked.

'Unfortunately for me, yes,' Mr Nickleby said. 'Both of them. And the mother, too. No money, and now they expect me to take care of them. They're all in London now, waiting for my help. What do I care about them? *I* never met them.'

Noggs looked at his employer's back with a strange **expression** on his face. It was not exactly a smile, but it was not a look of sadness either. Nobody could ever understand the expressions on Newman Noggs's face.

'Get me my coat and gloves, Newman,' Mr Nickleby suddenly decided, turning away from the window. 'I have a visit to make.'

Mr Nickleby walked quickly to the Strand, one of the busiest streets in London. He knocked several times on the door of a small house and waited. The door was finally opened by a servant girl.

'Is Mrs Nickleby at home?' he demanded.

'You mean Miss La Creevy?' the girl replied.

'No, I mean Mrs Nickleby!'

'Show the gentleman up, Hannah,' a voice called from inside the house.

Mr Nickleby walked straight past the servant girl into the hall of the house and quickly up the stairs. On the first floor he met a small, bird-like, middle-aged woman wearing black gloves and a yellow cloth tied around her head.

'My name's Miss La Creevy,' the woman said with a friendly smile. 'I'm an artist. Would you like me to paint your picture for you? You have a wonderfully serious face. Such strong eyes!'

'I'm not here for a painting, madam,' Mr Nickleby replied impatiently. 'I'm looking for a Mrs Nickleby. Is she here?'

---

yard /jɑːd/ (n) an area of land with a wall around it next to a building
expression /ɪkˈspreʃən/ (n) a look on someone's face

'A lady from the country and her two children have rented a room on the second floor,' the woman said. 'She's a **widow**.'

'A *poor* widow?'

'I'm afraid so.'

'That's her,' Mr Nickleby **sigh**ed.

widow /ˈwɪdəʊ/ (n) a woman whose husband has died
sigh /saɪ/ (v) to breathe out heavily when you are tired, bored or annoyed

The servant girl led him upstairs and into a small room. When he entered, a woman wearing a long black dress **rose** from her chair. A beautiful girl of about seventeen moved across the room to take her arm. A young man, two or three years older than his sister, stepped forwards and greeted Ralph as his uncle.

'You are Nicholas, I suppose?' Ralph said.

'That is my name, sir,' the young man smiled.

Ralph did not return his nephew's smile, but turned immediately to Mrs Nickleby. 'Well, madam, how are you?' he said. 'You must be brave in your sadness. I always am.'

'This is no ordinary sadness,' Mrs Nickleby said, putting her handkerchief to her eyes.

'I disagree,' Ralph said, calmly unbuttoning his coat. 'Husbands die every day, ma'am*, and wives, too.'

'And brothers also, sir,' Nicholas said, already beginning to dislike his uncle.

'Yes, sir, and dogs and cats,' Ralph replied, sitting down. 'You didn't say in your letter how my brother died, ma'am.'

'Nobody knows,' Mrs Nickleby said, her eyes filled with tears. 'We believe that he died of a broken heart.'

'Impossible!' Ralph said angrily. 'I can understand a broken neck or a broken leg, but not a broken heart. It is an excuse for people who want to escape their **debt**s.'

'Some people, I believe, have no hearts to break,' said Nicholas quietly.

Ralph turned round in his chair and looked at his nephew with **scorn**. 'How old is this boy?' he demanded.

'Nicholas is nearly nineteen,' said the widow.

'Nineteen, eh?' said Ralph. 'And do you have a job?'

'Not yet,' Nicholas answered proudly, 'but I'll find one.'

'You'd better,' Ralph said, staring at him with cold, grey eyes. 'You haven't got a penny in the world, have you?'

'That's true,' Nicholas said. 'But don't worry. I won't need *your* help.'

Nicholas's mother **beg**ged the emotional young man to control himself and asked Ralph to forgive her son for his rudeness.

---

* ma'am: a short form of 'madam'

rise /raɪz/ (v) to stand up
debt /det/ (n) borrowed money that you must pay back
scorn /skɔːn/ (n) an opinion or attitude that someone is stupid
beg /beg/ (v) to ask for something in an anxious away

Ralph gave Nicholas another scornful smile, then turned to Mrs Nickleby again. 'You say in your letter, ma'am, that my brother left you nothing when he died,' he said.

'That's true,' the widow said. 'I've had to sell our home to pay my husband's debts, and I've spent the last of my money on the journey to London. I hoped that you would be able to help your brother's children. That was his dying wish.'

'What can your daughter do, ma'am?' Ralph asked.

'She has learnt a little French and music.'

'And have you ever done anything?' Ralph said to Nicholas.

'No,' Nicholas replied.

'I thought not!' Ralph said, looking again at Mrs Nickleby. 'Your husband was a dreamer, ma'am. That's why he left you with no money, and left me with the problem of helping you. He was a foolish, selfish man.'

'Yes, that's true, I suppose,' Mrs Nickleby agreed. 'He never listened to my advice about money. I often think that I made a bad mistake when I married him ...'

Ralph listened to Mrs Nickleby's complaints about her husband with a half-smile. When she had finished, he looked at his nephew and said, 'Are you willing to work, sir?'

'Of course I am.'

'Then I have something here that may interest you.'

He took a newspaper from his pocket, and showed him an advertisement:

Mr Wackford Squeers's School for Boys, Dotheboys Hall, near Greta Bridge in Yorkshire, needs an assistant. He will be paid five pounds a year. Mr Squeers is staying in London, at the Saracen's Head Hotel, Snow Hill.

'Five pounds a year isn't much,' Kate complained. 'And Yorkshire is so far away!'

'Be quiet, dear,' Mrs Nickleby told her. 'I'm sure your uncle knows best.'

'And if I get this job,' Nicholas wanted to know, 'what will happen to my mother and sister?'

'I will take care of them,' Ralph promised. 'I will find your sister a job with a dressmaker that I know. But only if you take this job. Do you understand?'

'Then I agree,' Nicholas said, forgetting his anger of minutes earlier and shaking his uncle's hand. 'I'll take the job – if Mr Squeers will have me.'

'He will accept you – I can promise you that, ' Ralph said. 'Now, get your hat and coat, young man. We must go to the Saracen's Head immediately!'

CHAPTER 2

Dotheboys Hall

Nicholas's heart was filled with pity for these poor children,
who suffered such cruel treatment.

W ackford Squeers was a strange-looking man with flat, oily hair. His black jacket was much too big for him, and his trousers were much too short. But the strangest thing about him was his face. He only had one eye, which looked like a dirty window. When he smiled, it seemed to shine with a frightening green light.

At first, Mr Squeers was unwilling to accept Nicholas as his assistant because he was too young and had not been to college. But after a few quiet words with the boy's uncle, he offered Nicholas the job. 'The **coach** leaves at eight o'clock tomorrow morning,' he said. 'You mustn't be late.'

Nicholas woke up at six o'clock the next morning and hurried to the Saracen's Head. While he was helping Mr Squeers to lift a few small, frightened-looking boys onto the coach, he was surprised to see his mother and sister. His uncle had brought them to say goodbye.

'Why didn't you wake us?' Mrs Nickleby said, throwing her arms around her son. 'You left without breakfast!'

'There's no time for this, Nickleby!' Squeers interrupted rudely, buttoning his coat against the cold. 'Get onto the coach immediately. One of my boys has already nearly fallen off. If a boy died now, I'd lose twenty pounds!'

'Dear Nicholas,' whispered Kate, leading her brother away. 'What kind of place are you going to?'

'I don't know, Kate,' Nicholas replied, pressing his sister's hand. 'I suppose the people in Yorkshire are rougher than people in London.'

'He's a nasty little man. He's so rude.'

'But he's my employer,' Nicholas reminded her.

Nicholas kissed his tearful sister and mother and shook his uncle's hand. Then he jumped up into his seat on the coach.

However, as he was waving goodbye, an odd thing happened. Somebody started pulling softly at his leg. He looked down and saw a tall, thin man with strange, wild eyes.

'What's this?' Nicholas asked, when the man pushed a dirty letter into his hand.

coach /kəʊtʃ/ (n) a large, horse-pulled vehicle with a roof
however /haʊˈevə/ (adv) but; a word used to introduce a surprising fact or idea

7

'You don't know me,' the man whispered nervously, 'but I work for your uncle. Take it and read it.'

Before Nicholas could say another word, the man had gone.

The journey to Yorkshire was long and uncomfortable. It snowed heavily on the way, and everybody felt cold and hungry. At six o'clock the next evening, they finally arrived at Greta Bridge. Mr Squeers and Nicholas took the boys off the coach and put them into a small **cart**.

'Is it much further to Dotheboys Hall, sir?' Nicholas asked Squeers when the cart had left Greta Bridge.

'About three miles,' Squeers replied. 'But we don't call it a "Hall" up here – only in London, because it sounds better.'

Squeers laughed to himself, and Nicholas stared into the darkness until they reached Dotheboys Hall. Then he understood. The 'Hall' was just a long, low, cold-looking house with a few old farm buildings behind it.

cart /kɑːt/ (n) a small wooden vehicle that is pulled by a horse

While Nicholas sat in the cart with the boys, Squeers jumped down and shouted for someone to open the gate. Several minutes later, a tall boy in old, thin clothes ran out of the house.

'Why did you take so long, Smike?' Squeers shouted.

'Sorry, sir, but I fell asleep by the fire.'

'Fire? What fire?' the **schoolmaster** demanded angrily.

'Mrs Squeers said that I could sit by the fire in the kitchen to keep warm.'

'Mrs Squeers is a fool,' Squeers replied. 'You'd stay awake better in the cold!'

The boy called Smike opened the gate, looking nervously at Squeers. A few minutes later, Nicholas was standing outside the door with the boys and the luggage. He stared up at the cold-looking house with its dark windows and sighed. He was a long way from his home and family, and he had never felt so lonely.

schoolmaster /ˈskuːlˌmɑːstə/ (n) a teacher in a school

Life at Dotheboys Hall was very hard. There was no heating in the school, and the boys had to wash with buckets of icy water in the mornings. They wore the same clothes every day, and they were always hungry. Mrs Squeers fed them a thick, horrible soup every day which Mr Squeers called their 'medicine'. It was the cheapest food that they could find.

The classroom was cold and dirty with broken windows. There were a couple of old, long desks for the children, and two desks at the front of the room – one for Squeers, and a smaller one for his assistant. During the lessons, the boys sat quietly, shaking with the cold. Letters from home were opened in front of the whole class and Squeers took all their money. He did the same with packages of clothes. If the boys complained, Squeers hit them with a big stick. Nicholas watched this happen with tears of anger in his eyes, but he felt powerless to do anything.

Squeers gave to his son, young Wackford, all the clothes that he stole from the boys. He, of course, was the only boy in the school who was never cold and hungry. He was also as nasty as his father. His favourite activity was kicking the other boys and making them cry. If they tried to defend themselves, young Wackford reported them to his father and they were cruelly punished.

Nicholas's heart was filled with pity for these poor children, who suffered such cruel **treat**ment. All the beauty of innocence had disappeared from their pale, thin faces. He never heard them laughing, and there was no hope in their dull, empty eyes.

He was especially sorry for the boy called Smike. He was older than the other boys – about eighteen or nineteen years old. He was tall for his age but wore children's clothes that were much too short for him. He did not have lessons, but was made to do all the hard, dirty jobs around the school. If he did something wrong, Mr Squeers beat him and shouted at him. Smike had been left at the school many years earlier by parents who did not want him. However, Squeers still received money for him from somewhere. He kept him at the school because he was useful.

One evening, Nicholas sat on his hard, wooden bed in the crowded, unheated room that he shared with several other boys. He was thinking sadly of home when suddenly he remembered the letter which the man with wild eyes had given him. He took it out of his pocket and read:

My dear young man, I know the world. Your father did not, and you do not either. If you knew the world, you would not go on this journey. If you ever want help in London (don't be angry), go to the Crown Hotel, in Golden

treat /triːt/ (v) to behave towards someone in the way that is described

Square. They will give you my address. You can come at night. Many years ago, people were not ashamed to know me. Now things are different – but that is not important. There is no future. Newman Noggs.

While Nicholas was putting the letter back in his pocket, a strange thing happened to him. His eyes filled with tears.

The next day, Nicholas saw Smike on his knees, trying to light a fire. Smike looked up at Nicholas with a frightened expression.

'Don't be afraid, ' Nicholas said kindly. 'I'm not going to hurt you. Are you cold?'

Smike covered his face with his thin, dirty hands and started crying. 'My heart will break if I stay in this horrible place,' he said. 'Before you arrived, a boy died here. He was my last friend. Just before he died, his face was lit up by a lovely smile. He said that he could see the faces of his friends around his bed. They had come from home and they were smiling and talking to him. What faces will smile at me when I die? There's no hope for me, alive or dead. No hope.'

'There's always hope,' Nicholas said gently, resting his hand on the boy's bony shoulder.

Eventually, Smike stopped crying and moved away, like a frightened animal, into the shadows. Nicholas sighed sadly and went to bed.

2.1 Were you right?

Look back at your answers to Activity 1.2 on page iv. Are they true or false? Give reasons.

1 ....

2 ....

3 ....

4 ....

2.2 What more did you learn?

Answer the questions.

1 Who are these people? Write their names.

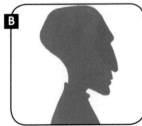

....

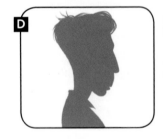

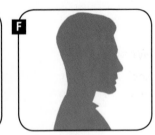

....

2 Which of the people above are described here? Write the letters.

☐ tall, thin and afraid   ☐ rich and selfish

☐ strange-looking but kind   ☐ ugly and cruel

3 Which words (✓ or ✗) describe Nicholas? Give a reason for each answer.

☐ emotional ....
☐ grateful ....
☐ lonely ....
☐ proud ....

.3 Language in use

Look at the sentence on the right. Then write the correct form of the words in the boxes in these sentences.

> Her eyes were filled with **sadness** (sad).

1 Noggs had a strange .... on his face. | express |

2 'Forgive my son for his ....' | rude |

3 Ralph listened to Mrs Nickleby's .... | complain |

4 The children suffered from .... | angry |

5 There were tears of .... in his eyes. | hungry |

6 The children suffered such cruel .... | treat |

.4 What's next?

Look at the start of Chapter 3 and the words in italics. Then look at the pictures on pages 15, 17 and 20. What (✓) is going to happen?

1 ☐ Nicholas will fall in love.
2 ☐ Fanny will have a fight with her friend.
3 ☐ Wackford Squeers will treat Smike more kindly.
4 ☐ Nicholas will make new friends at Dotheboys Hall.
5 ☐ Smike will become Nicholas's enemy.
6 ☐ Newman Noggs will visit Nicholas at Dotheboys Hall.

Fanny Squeers

'When did he ask you to marry him?'
'Oh, he hasn't asked me yet,' Fanny said.

Wackford Squeers had a twenty-two-year-old daughter, Fanny, who was short and ugly, like her father. One evening, she was having dinner with her parents while they were discussing Nicholas. Fanny had never met Nicholas because she was staying with her friend Tilda when he arrived. She therefore listened to her parents' conversation with interest. When she heard her father say that he was the 'son of a gentleman', she became *very* interested!

Later that night, she asked her servant about the new teacher. She heard that he had beautiful dark eyes, long straight legs and a sweet smile. She decided that she wanted to meet this interesting young man as soon as possible.

The next day, she went into the schoolroom, pretending that she needed a pen. When she saw Nicholas, her face went red. 'I'm sorry,' she said. 'I thought my father was here. Oh, how embarrassing!'

'Mr Squeers is out,' Nicholas explained politely.

'Could you lend me a pen?' the young lady asked, looking shyly at her feet. 'He *does* have a beautiful smile,' she thought, giving him a secret, sideways look.

Nicholas gave her a pen, and Fanny left the classroom. Outside the door, she held the pen to her heart. 'I've never seen such wonderful legs!' she sighed, walking away in a dream. Minutes later, she put on her hat and coat and hurried out of the school. 'I have to tell Tilda about him,' she thought.

Fanny was jealous of Tilda Price, who was five years younger than her. A week earlier a farmer, John Browdie, had asked Tilda to marry him. 'Now I can tell her that *I'm* going to get married, too!' Fanny thought.

Tilda was surprised when she heard Fanny's news. 'This is wonderful!' she said. 'When did he ask you to marry him?'

'Oh, he hasn't asked me yet,' Fanny said. 'But I know that he wants to. He smiles at me in a *very* special way.'

'Oh, Fanny,' Tilda said, **hug**ging her friend. 'I'm so happy for you. When can I meet the lucky young man?'

'In two days' time, my parents are away on business. Then you and John can both come for tea.'

'What a lovely idea!' Tilda said excitedly. 'I can't wait!'

Two days later, Tilda arrived early at Dotheboys Hall. 'John will be here later,' she explained. 'He's gone home to wash and change his clothes.'

hug /hʌg/ (v) to hold someone tightly in a friendly way

The two girls helped each other with their hair and clothes, then went downstairs. While Fanny was talking excitedly about her 'future husband', there was a knock on the door.

'Come in,' Fanny called nervously.

'Good evening …' Nicholas said, a look of surprise on his face. He had expected to find Mr Squeers.

'Father can't be with us today,' Fanny said. 'But that only makes it better for us, doesn't it?'

Nicholas thought that these words were strange, but he paid no attention to them. He greeted Tilda politely, and stood calmly by the window.

'Don't be embarrassed,' Tilda said, smiling at him. 'I don't mind what you two do in front of me. You can pretend that I'm not here!'

'Tilda!' Fanny said, her face going red.

The two girls started laughing. Nicholas thought that the girls' behaviour was so silly that he started laughing, too.

Soon, the three of them were sitting happily at the table, eating bread and butter and drinking tea. Ten minutes later, John Browdie arrived. He was a big, strong man, but he was not very good at conversation. He seemed happy just to eat bread and butter.

When the plates were empty, John stared at Nicholas and said, 'You're a lucky man to have bread and butter here.'

'What do you mean, sir?' Nicholas replied.

'The last teacher nearly died of hunger,' John laughed. 'Mr Squeers doesn't like spending money!'

Nicholas went red with anger and he told Mr Browdie to apologise for his rudeness in front of Mr Squeers's daughter. Tilda was angry, too.

'If you say another word, John,' she said, 'I'll never speak to you again!' Then she turned to Nicholas and whispered, 'John and I will go into the kitchen. We'll leave you two alone for a few minutes.'

'Why do you want to do that?' Nicholas asked, confused.

'Mr Nickleby, I'm shocked! Look at poor Miss Squeers. She was so excited about today, and she's dressed so prettily because of you.'

'Because of me? Why?'

Tilda looked at Nicholas with a strange smile. 'Does this handsome man think that I'm more beautiful than Fanny?' she thought. 'Perhaps he doesn't want to marry her now.'

'Let's have a game of cards,' she said suddenly.

'There are only four of us, Tilda,' Fanny said, looking at Nicholas out of the corner of her eye. 'We'd better play with partners, hadn't we? Two against two.'

'What do you think, Mr Nickleby?' Tilda asked.

'I'll be happy to be your partner, Miss Price,' Nicholas replied.

'Mr Browdie,' Fanny said, looking at Tilda angrily. 'Will you be *my* partner?'

John Browdie agreed, although he could not understand why Fanny seemed so upset.

'We're going to win everything,' Nicholas said cheerfully, after he and Tilda had won the first game.

'I think Tilda has already won something that she didn't expect – haven't you, dear?' Fanny said nastily.

'Only a game of cards, my dear,' Tilda replied, pretending not to understand. She was enjoying Fanny's jealousy.

'How boring you are tonight!' Fanny said with a bitter smile.

'Not at all,' Tilda replied. 'I'm in an excellent mood. I was thinking that *you* seemed unusually boring tonight.'

'Me!' Fanny cried, biting her lip and shaking jealously.

'And your hair's beginning to look untidy,' Tilda said.

The two friends' argument became worse and worse. Finally, Fanny started crying. 'Tilda, I hate you,' she shouted.

'I feel the same way about you,' Tilda said.

John Browdie hit the table hard with his enormous hand. 'I've had enough!' he shouted. 'I'm going home!'

'Me, too,' Tilda said, standing up and putting on her hat. She hurried out of the room, followed by John Browdie.

Nicholas looked at Fanny. He was unsure of what to do. Fanny was crying into her handkerchief, shouting things at the closed door. After a few minutes, he quietly left the room.

'In a horrible place like this, I need all the friends I can get,' he said to himself. 'But instead, I only seem to make enemies. What have I done?'

With these unhappy thoughts, he climbed into his dirty, cold bed. But as he lay awake, listening to the other boys in their beds crying with cold and hunger, he soon forgot his own problems. 'Why do places as terrible as this exist?' he thought angrily. 'These poor children are treated worse than animals. Why do their families send them here?'

The next day, things became even worse. When it became clear that Nicholas did not love her, Fanny was filled with anger and confusion. She could not understand why a poor teacher like him did not find her attractive. In addition to this, he had embarrassed her in front of her friend. This showed that Nicholas was not grateful to her father for giving him a job. 'Well,' she thought, 'he has an enemy instead of a friend. I'm going to make life very difficult for him.'

She noticed that Smike seemed to like Nicholas a lot. He followed the young teacher everywhere, and was happy just to be near him. Fanny complained about this to her father, who began to treat Smike even more roughly than before.

One January morning, Smike disappeared. Squeers and his wife went out to look for him, and eventually found him several miles away by the side of the road. He was covered in mud, frozen, tired and hungry. They tied his hands and feet together and brought him back to the school. Then Squeers ordered everybody to go to the schoolroom. He pulled Smike into the room and threw him onto the floor.

'Have you anything to say?' Squeers said to Smike, lifting a stick above his head.

'Please don't hit me, sir,' Smike cried.

Squeers laughed, and brought the stick down hard on the boy's back. Smike screamed with pain while the other boys watched silently. Squeers lifted the stick again, but a loud voice shouted, 'Stop!'

'Who said that?' demanded Squeers, turning round angrily.

'I did,' said Nicholas.

'Sit down!' Squeers told him angrily.

He lifted his stick to hit Smike again, but Nicholas moved quickly towards him.

'I warn you not to touch him,' he said. 'I've seen enough of your **evil** school and your treatment of the children here.'

Without warning, Squeers screamed wildly and hit Nicholas across the face with his stick. Nicholas immediately jumped on Squeers, took the stick from his hand and began to hit him. Mrs Squeers and Fanny tried to pull Nicholas away, but Nicholas was too strong for them all. He pushed them off and threw the schoolmaster across the room. Squeers hit the wall hard and sank to the floor without moving.

evil /ˈiːvəl/ (adj) very cruel or harmful

Nicholas looked around, but he could not see Smike. After a moment's thought, he decided that he had no choice. He had to leave the school immediately. He packed his bag quickly and marched out of the front door into the snow.

After walking for a few miles, he calmed down and thought about his situation more clearly. He did not know how he was going to get to London. He only had a little money, and London was over two hundred and fifty miles away.

While Nicholas was worrying about this, he noticed a man on a horse riding towards him. It was John Browdie. They exchanged greetings but did not smile.

After a few seconds' silence, Nicholas said, 'I'm very sorry about our argument. It was my fault. Will you shake hands?'

John Browdie jumped down from his horse with a big smile and shook hands. Then he noticed the cuts on Nicholas's face. When Nicholas told him what had happened, he laughed and shook his hand again.

'You've beaten the schoolmaster?' he said. 'That's the best thing I've heard for years! I love you for it!'

But he became more serious when Nicholas told him about his plan to walk to London. He pulled an old purse out of his pocket and gave Nicholas enough money for the coach journey. Nicholas tried to refuse, but John Browdie did not listen.

'Good luck, young man,' he said, when Nicholas had finally accepted the money. With a cheerful wave, he climbed back onto his horse and rode away, laughing loudly.

Nicholas continued his journey, but he did not travel far that afternoon. It was nearly dark and there had been a heavy fall of snow, so he went into an empty farmhouse and fell asleep.

When he woke up the next morning, he saw a dark shape sitting in front of him. It was Smike!

'What are you doing here?' Nicholas asked with surprise.

'I want to go with you,' the boy replied. 'You're the only friend I have. Please take me with you.'

'I'm as poor and lonely as you are,' Nicholas said. 'How can I help *you*?'

'Please!' the boy begged. 'I'll be your servant. I won't ask for anything. I only want to be near you.'

Nicholas agreed, and Smike's face lit up with happiness. He did not know where they were going, but he did not care. He was with his friend, and away from Dotheboys Hall. That was enough to fill his heart with happiness.

CHAPTER 4

Return to London

*'Will you, sir, return that boy to the school where
he belongs?' 'I will not.'*

Newman Noggs had **lodgings** at the top of a house near Golden Square.
Arriving home from work one night, he saw two tired, wet travellers
waiting patiently outside his door. He invited them straight in and gave them
some hot soup and some dry clothes.

'I read your letter,' Nicholas explained as the three of them sat around the fire.
'I got your address from the Crown Hotel, as you suggested. Tell me, how are my
mother and sister?'

'Well. Your uncle is letting them live in an empty old house that belongs to
him. It's near the river, and it was in a terrible condition when they first moved
in. It was smelly and dirty, with rats everywhere.' A strange expression crossed his
face when he said this. Nicholas did not know whether Newman felt amused or
sickened. 'But your mother and sister have cleaned a couple of rooms and made
them quite comfortable,' Newman continued, noticing the anxious look on
Nicholas's face. 'And they don't have to pay any rent.'

Nicholas looked **relieved**. 'I wanted to come here before visiting them,' he
explained. 'I didn't want to cause them any unnecessary problems.' He then
described his recent adventures at Dotheboys Hall.

lodgings /ˈlɒdʒɪŋz/ (n) a room or rooms in someone's house for paying guests
relieved /rɪˈliːvd/ (adj) pleased that something bad has not happened

When he had finished, Newman looked at him seriously. 'My dear young man,' he said, 'you'll never make progress in the world if you behave like that … but I'm proud of you!'

'Has my uncle heard about it yet?' Nicholas asked. Newman opened and shut his mouth several times, but did not say anything. 'I must know the bad news sooner or later,' Nicholas said. 'Please tell me now.'

Newman rose from his chair and took a piece of paper from a drawer. It was a copy of a letter which Ralph had received from Fanny Squeers two days earlier. In it, she described how Nicholas had attacked her father, stolen a valuable ring and run away with Smike – 'an evil, ungrateful boy'.

'She's lying,' Nicholas said angrily. 'I must find my uncle and tell him what *really* happened.'

'Your uncle's out of town,' Newman replied. 'He won't be back for three days. He won't answer this letter before he returns. Don't worry. Nobody else knows about it.'

'Are you sure? Not even my mother and sister? Then I must go and see them.'

'No, you mustn't,' Newman said. 'Speak to your uncle when he returns.'

The next day, Nicholas found small, cheap lodgings for himself and Smike, and immediately started looking for a job. He went to a small but busy job **agency** near Oxford Street, in the centre of London, where he was offered work as a French teacher for the daughters of a local businessman. Nicholas accepted the job happily. As he was walking out, a girl of about eighteen years old came in from the street. He stood to one side as she shyly walked past him. She was so beautiful that he stood and watched her for a long time. He had never seen such a lovely, innocent face, although there was something sad about her soft blue eyes. Eventually, he turned away and walked home, unable to stop thinking about her.

Two days later, Nicholas went to visit his uncle, who had just returned to London. His uncle was not at home, so he went instead to see Miss La Creevy.

'Mr Nicholas!' Miss La Creevy cried happily when she saw him at her door. 'Come in. You must join me for breakfast. You look so thin, and your face is so pale.'

While they were having breakfast, Miss La Creevy asked him why he had returned to London. Nicholas explained to her what had happened. Then he said, 'I came here because I want to see my uncle. I have to **persuade** him that I'm not a thief. I went to his house this morning, but he wasn't at home. I must see him before he tells my mother and sister these lies about me. Perhaps you can help me.'

agency /'eɪdʒənsi/ (n) a business that arranges services for people
persuade /pə'sweɪd/ (v) to make someone decide to do something

'How can I do that?' Miss La Creevy asked, looking worried.

'My mother and sister don't know that I've returned from Yorkshire. Could you show me where they live? I want to see them before my uncle does.'

Miss La Creevy took him straight to the house by the river, and Nicholas was shocked when he saw it. Its windows were covered with mud, and its walls were wet and dirty. It had probably been empty for many years. Miss La Creevy led him through the door, across a dark, smelly hall and up some stairs. She stopped outside a freshly painted door.

'This is it,' she said. 'Your mother and I have worked very hard to make this as comfortable as possible.'

However, as she was going to knock on the door, she stopped. There was the sound of a man's deep voice from inside the room. Ralph Nickleby had arrived before them!

He was telling Mrs Nickleby and Kate about Nicholas, and they were both crying.

'It's impossible!' Kate said. 'Nicholas isn't a thief. Mother, how can you sit and listen to such things?'

Mrs Nickleby, who had never been very good at understanding situations, just cried even more loudly into her handkerchief.

'If my nephew's innocent, why is he hiding from us?' Ralph said. 'I'm afraid you must both accept the fact that he's a dangerous criminal.'

'That's a lie!' an angry voice shouted, and Nicholas rushed in.

Ralph turned and stared angrily at his nephew.

'Dear Nicholas,' Kate cried, throwing her arms around her brother. 'Be calm, don't do anything foolish …'

'Be calm?' Nicholas replied, his face red with anger. 'How can I be calm in front of this man? He sent me to an evil place to work for the cruellest man that I've ever known. And now he's poisoning the ears of my family against me …'

'Be patient,' Kate begged him. 'Calm down. Tell us what really happened.'

'It's true that I attacked the schoolmaster,' Nicholas said. 'But I did it to save a poor, innocent boy from certain death. I'm not sorry. I'd do the same again if I had the chance.'

'Do you hear this?' Ralph said, turning to Mrs Nickleby. 'Your son isn't even sorry!'

'Oh dear!' cried Mrs Nickleby. 'I don't know what to think.'

'But I'm not a thief!' Nicholas continued, staring proudly at his uncle. 'I found a ring in my pocket after I'd left that horrible school. It was a cheap ring.

I believe that Mrs Squeers put it there to make me look like a thief. I sent it back to the school immediately.'

'And what about the boy, Smike?' Kate asked. 'Is it true that you ran away with him?'

'Yes. He's the boy that I saved from the schoolmaster. He's suffered years of cruel treatment at that school. He wanted to come with me, and he's with me now.'

'So everything *is* true,' Ralph said. 'You don't deny it! Will you, sir, return that boy to the school where he belongs?'

'I will not.'

'You refuse?' said Ralph. 'Then you must listen to me.'

'Why? I will not listen to any more of your lies.'

'Then I will speak to your mother. She understands the real world. Ma'am, I tried to help you by finding your son honest work, but he is a lazy, selfish, ungrateful boy. I will not help him – or you, if he stays with you. If that boy stays, I will leave you now. You will never see me again.'

'You've been kind to us, sir,' Mrs Nickleby replied from behind her handkerchief. 'But I can't send my own son away, even if he is guilty of these terrible crimes.'

'Why do you say "if", Mother?' Kate asked. 'You know he's innocent.'

'I don't know what to think,' Mrs Nickleby replied. 'Nicholas is sometimes very bad-tempered, and your uncle has been so good to us. But let's not talk about it any more. I can't send my own son away. Even if it means that we don't have a penny in the world …'

Ralph turned towards the door, but Nicholas stopped him. 'You needn't leave this place, sir,' he said. 'I'll go, and you won't see me for a very long time.'

'Nicholas!' Kate said, throwing her arms again around her brother. 'You can't go. You'll break my heart if you do.'

'I have to,' Nicholas replied gently. 'If I stay, I'll only bring you unhappiness. We won't forget each other, I promise. And I'm sure that better days will come.'

He kissed his sister gently, then turned again to his uncle. 'I leave my family to you, sir,' he whispered. 'But I promise – if anything bad happens to them, you'll be punished.'

Nicholas left the room without another word and, a few days later, he and Smike left London.

Activities 3

3.1 Were you right?

Look back at your answers to Activity 2.4. Then match the first parts of these sentences with their endings, A–F.

1 ☐ Fanny pretends to need a pen because she
2 ☐ Fanny is jealous because her friend
3 ☐ Squeers hits Smike because he
4 ☐ John Browdie is friendly because Nicholas
5 ☐ Nicholas is surprised because Smike
6 ☐ Nicholas visits Newman Noggs when he

A ... apologises for the argument.
B .... tried to run away.
C .... wants to meet Nicholas.
D .... arrives in London.
E .... has followed him to an empty farmhouse.
F .... is going to get married.

3.2 What more did you learn?

Complete these sentences with the names in the box.

> Miss La Creevy   Kate Nickleby   Smike   Mrs Nickleby   Fanny Squeers
> Ralph Nickleby   Newman Noggs   John Browdie

1 .... tells lies about Nicholas.

2 .... gives Nicholas some money.

3 .... goes to London with Nicholas.

4 .... gives Nicholas news about his family.

5 .... takes Nicholas to a house by the river.

6 Nicholas refuses to obey ....

7 .... doesn't believe her brother is a thief.

8 .... refuses to send Nicholas away.

3 Language in use

Look at the sentence on the right. Then look at the pictures below. What did these people ask?

> Miss La Creevy asked him **why he had returned** to London.

> Could you lend me a pen?

> When can I meet the lucky young man?

> Have you anything to say?

1

2

3

Fanny asked Nicholas
if he could lend her
a pen.

Tilda asked Fanny
....
....
....

Squeers asked Smike
....
....
....

> What are you doing here?

> Did you run away with Smike?

4

5

Nicholas asked Smike
....
....

Kate asked Nicholas
....
....

.4 What's next?

Look at the pictures in the next chapter and the words in *italics* on page 26. What problems do you think Kate will have while Nicholas is away? Make notes.

Notes

CHAPTER 5

Sir Mulberry Hawk

'Let me go immediately, sir,' Kate whispered angrily.
'My dear girl, why do you pretend to dislike me so much?'

Soon after Nicholas had left London, Kate lost her job at the dressmaker's. Her mother looked through the newspapers and quickly found an interesting advertisement: a woman called Mrs Wititterly was looking for a **companion**. Although Kate did not really want the job, she was too tired and upset by recent events to argue. She went with her mother for an interview with Mrs Wititterly.

Mrs Wititterly – a nervous, ill-looking woman – lived in a large house near Sloane Square, a very expensive part of London. Kate's gentleness and intelligence pleased her, and she offered Kate the job as her companion.

Mrs Nickleby was very excited. 'Mrs Wititterly looks very ill,' she thought. 'Perhaps she'll die soon and Mr Wititterly – a fine-looking gentleman! – will fall in love with Kate. He'll ask her to marry him and all our troubles will end!'

A week after the interview, Kate moved all her things to Mrs Wititterly's house and started work.

Ralph Nickleby had a very important business customer, Sir Mulberry Hawk, an ugly old man with lots of money, who had met Kate once at dinner at Ralph's house. Unfortunately for Kate, this horrible old man had liked her a lot. He had sat next to her at dinner and had embarrassed her all evening with his rude jokes and horrible wet-lipped smiles. She had been so upset by his impolite behaviour that she had left the table. After dinner, Sir Mulberry had told Ralph that he wanted to meet Kate again. He asked Ralph to help him and Ralph agreed immediately, thinking that this would be good for his business.

He arranged for Sir Mulberry to meet Mrs Nickleby at his office. Mrs Nickleby liked Sir Mulberry because he said so many nice things about her and her daughter.

'Such a beautiful, intelligent girl!' he said. 'But I'm not surprised. She has such a beautiful, intelligent mother.'

Mrs Nickleby smiled proudly, and let Sir Mulberry walk home with her.

When he had said goodbye, she closed her eyes with excitement. 'I don't believe it,' she thought. 'Such a fine gentleman! He will be an even better husband for Kate than Mr Wititterly!'

One evening, Sir Mulberry invited Mrs Nickleby to the theatre with him. She put on her best clothes and sat with him in the most expensive seats.

companion /kəmˈpænjən/ (n) someone who you spend a lot of time with

Sir Mulberry was a drunk, but Mrs Nickleby did not care. She felt proud to be with such a well-dressed gentleman – especially as he was so interested in her daughter.

He was telling her for the twentieth time how beautiful Kate was when suddenly he stopped. 'Listen!' he said. 'Some people have come into the next seats. I'm sure I recognise one of the voices.'

Mrs Nickleby listened, and opened her mouth with surprise. She bent forwards and looked around the curtain between the seats. 'Kate!' she said. 'What a lovely surprise!'

'Mother!' Kate replied, equally surprised. 'What are *you* doing here?' Then she noticed a man sitting in the shadows behind her mother. He was smiling at Kate and kissing the back of his hand.

'Who is that man with you?' Kate whispered.

'You'll never guess!' replied Mrs Nickleby loudly, so that Mrs Wititterly could hear. 'This is Sir Mulberry Hawk.'

Kate remembered the horrible old man from her uncle's dinner party, and her face went pale. However, Mrs Nickleby mistook the strange look on her daughter's face for shyness – the shyness of love!

Mrs Wititterly was as excited as Mrs Nickleby, because Sir Mulberry Hawk was such an important gentleman. She told her husband to invite Sir Mulberry and Mrs Nickleby to sit with them.

'Dear Kate,' said Mrs Nickleby, kissing her daughter. 'How ill you looked a moment ago! You frightened me!'

'It was nothing, Mother,' Kate replied, but it was too late to explain her true feelings to her.

She greeted Sir Mulberry politely, then turned her head towards the stage. Sir Mulberry sat behind her all evening, and she could not enjoy the play. When the play had finished, Sir Mulberry took her arm. Kate tried to escape and walk away, but Sir Mulberry pulled her back.

'Don't hurry,' he said.

'Let me go immediately, sir,' Kate whispered angrily.

'My dear girl, why do you pretend to dislike me so much?'

'*Pretend!*' Kate repeated. 'How impolite of you, sir, to talk to me in this way!'

'You look prettier when you're angry,' Sir Mulberry said, moving his face closer to hers.

'I hate you, sir,' Kate said, pulling back from him. 'You show scorn for my feelings. If you do not let me join my friends immediately, you'll be sorry. I can be rude, too. I know how to embarrass a man like you in public.'

Sir Mulberry smiled, but did not let go of her arm. When they had reached the front of the theatre, Kate pulled away from him angrily. She hurried past her mother and the Wititterlys without a word. Then she jumped into the waiting **carriage**, threw herself into the darkest corner and cried.

The next day, Kate received a long letter from her mother, congratulating her on her choice of future husband! Kate felt more upset than ever, but she had to try to forget her unhappiness. Her job was to be cheerful with Mrs Wititterly.

That afternoon, while she was reading to her employer, there was a knock on the door.

'That's Sir Mulberry Hawk,' Mrs Wititterly smiled from her sofa. 'I gave him permission to visit. Aren't you pleased?'

carriage /ˈkærɪdʒ/ (n) a vehicle that is pulled by a horse

Before Kate could answer, the door opened and Sir Mulberry walked into the room. He sat with the two ladies for over an hour. Mr Wititterly sat with them, too, enjoying the visit of such an important guest. But Kate refused to be friendly.

Sir Mulberry seemed to find Kate's unfriendliness attractive, and he visited the house every day for the next two weeks. However, as his feelings for Kate became clearer, there was a change in Mrs Wititterly's behaviour. Jealous of the attention that he gave to Kate, she became less friendly towards her.

Poor Kate had never been so sad. She already had to suffer Sir Mulberry Hawk's visits every afternoon. Now she had to suffer Mrs Wititterly's increasing coldness towards her, too. Eventually, the two women had a big argument, and Kate hurried to her uncle's house.

Ralph Nickleby was counting money in his office when his niece arrived. He quickly hid the money, put an empty purse on his desk and told Newman Noggs to show her in.

'Well, my dear, what's the matter now?' he asked.

Her eyes shone with anger as she told him about Sir Mulberry. 'He's such a rude, unpleasant man,' she said. 'Mother thinks that he's a gentleman, but she's wrong. Why did you allow him to meet me in this way?'

Something about her proud expression reminded Ralph of Nicholas. 'There is some of that boy's blood in you, I see,' he said.

'I hope there is!' replied Kate. 'And I'm proud of it. As I am your brother's child, I *will not* accept these insults any more.'

'What insults, girl?'

'That man treats me like a toy. Uncle, you have to stop him. I'm sure that you will help me. I have no one to advise me or protect me except for you. Please help me.'

'How can I help you, child?' Ralph said, rising from his chair and walking up and down behind his desk.

'Tell him to leave me alone.'

'No,' Ralph shook his head. 'I can't do that.' Kate looked at him in surprise. 'He's an important customer. I can't afford to offend him. You'll have to live with it. He'll soon get bored with you. Just be patient ...'

'Patient!' Kate cried. 'I'd rather live on the street than have to see that man again.'

Before Ralph could say another word, she left the room. As she was closing the door behind her, she was surprised to find Newman Noggs standing in the hall.

'I heard everything,' he said. 'You're right to be strong in front of him. Oh, yes! Ha-ha-ha! Oh, yes, you poor thing.' He walked slowly across the hall and opened the door to let her out into the street. 'Don't be sad,' he whispered. 'I shall see you soon. Ha-ha-ha. And so will somebody else. Yes, yes.'

'Thank you,' Kate answered, hurrying past him. 'You're very kind.'

She walked quickly back to Mrs Wititterly's house, trying to understand Newman's strange words. She did not know that Newman had received a letter from Nicholas. Her brother and Smike were working for a small theatre company in the south of England. Newman knew Nicholas's address, and planned to write to him about Kate's problems as soon as he could.

CHAPTER 6

Nicholas Fights Back

Nicholas's anger was greater than his pain, and he threw himself at Sir Mulberry.

When Nicholas received Newman's letter, he and Smike returned to London immediately. They went straight to Newman's lodgings, but the clerk was not at home. Nicholas left Smike to wait for him, and went to see Miss La Creevy, who was not at home either.

After thinking for a moment, he decided to see his mother. A servant girl told him that Mrs Nickleby was at the theatre for the evening. She also told him that his sister now lived at a different address.

Nicholas walked anxiously along the streets, wondering what to do. Feeling hungry, he stopped outside a handsome hotel. 'An expensive place,' he thought. 'But a glass of wine and a piece of cake will not cost too much.'

He went into the hotel and entered the coffee-room. It was empty except for a noisy group of four gentlemen at one table. Nicholas sat down at a table near the fire, ordered some wine and cake, and began to read a newspaper. Suddenly, he heard one of the men at the other table say his sister's name, and looked up from his paper with surprise.

'Little Kate Nickleby!' the other three men said, lifting their glasses.

The four men drank their wine, put their empty glasses on the table and started laughing.

Nicholas's face burned with anger, but he did not move.

'She's a clever little thing,' the first man said. 'She pretends that she doesn't like me, but she's only playing a game. She's like her uncle.'

'Perhaps her mother is jealous,' another man said. 'She's locked her daughter up. That's why you can't see her.'

'That's no problem,' the first man said. 'I can do anything with the old lady. She'll believe anything I tell her.'

The four men started laughing again.

Nicholas rose angrily and walked across to their table. 'I'd like to speak to you, sir,' he said, staring at the man who had spoken last.

'With me, sir?' Sir Mulberry Hawk replied, looking at Nicholas with drunken scorn.

'With you, sir, in private,' Nicholas replied quietly.

'A mysterious stranger!' Sir Mulberry laughed, lifting his wine-glass to his thick, ugly lips and looking round at his friends.

'Do you refuse to speak to me?' Nicholas said.

'Tell me what you want or go away,' Sir Mulberry answered, drinking more wine.

Nicholas took a card from his pocket and threw it on the table. 'There, sir,' he said. 'You will know what I want when you see my name.'

Sir Mulberry read the name on the card, threw it back onto the table and continued drinking.

'Your name and address, sir?' Nicholas said quietly, shaking with anger.

'I shall give you neither,' replied Sir Mulberry.

'If you are not a gentleman, sir, perhaps one of your friends is. Can anybody give me this man's name and address?' There was silence around the table. 'I am the brother of the young lady who has been the subject of conversation at this table,' Nicholas said. 'This man is a lying coward. If no one will tell me his name or address, I can easily discover it.'

Sir Mulberry looked at Nicholas with scorn, then said to his friends, 'Let him talk until midnight if he wants. I have nothing serious to say to a boy of his low class.'

The four men continued laughing and drinking, so Nicholas returned to his table and waited. Eventually, three of the men went home, leaving Sir Mulberry alone in the room with Nicholas.

Sir Mulberry sat in silence, staring at the wall with drunken, empty eyes. Nicholas watched and waited, but said nothing. At last, Sir Mulberry gave Nicholas another long, scornful look and rose slowly to his feet. With the waiter's help, he put on his gloves, hat and coat. Then he walked outside.

Nicholas followed him into the street. 'Will you tell me who you are?' he said again.

'No.'

'I shall hold on to your carriage if you don't tell me.'

'I shall tell my driver to hit you if you do.'

'You're an evil man.'

'And what are you?'

'I'm the son of a country gentleman,' Nicholas replied. 'I'm the same as you in birth and background, and better than you in everything else. I tell you again, Miss Nickleby is my sister. Will you or will you not tell me who you are?'

'I'd tell a real gentleman, but not a boy like you. Get out of my way, dog!'

Sir Mulberry pushed him to one side and got into his carriage. Nicholas jumped forward and put his hands on the door.

'I will not let you leave until you …'

Before he could finish his sentence, Sir Mulberry lifted his stick and hit him hard on the side of the head. Nicholas's anger was greater than his pain, and he threw himself at Sir Mulberry. In the fight that followed, he managed to take hold of the stick and hit Sir Mulberry across the face with its heavy handle. Sir Mulberry fell back into the carriage and Nicholas fell to the ground. Frightened by the fighting, the horse ran off wildly down the street, pulling the carriage behind it.

Nicholas felt sick, but he rose painfully to his feet. There was loud shouting all around him as the driver and other men ran after the carriage. As soon as the carriage disappeared around a corner, there was a loud crash, a scream and the sound of breaking glass.

When Nicholas arrived back at the lodgings, he found Newman Noggs sitting by the fire with Smike.

'What have you been doing?' Newman asked when he saw Nicholas's blood-covered face.

'Don't worry about me,' Nicholas replied. 'I'm not badly hurt. But I want you to tell me about my sister. I've learnt part of the story tonight. You must tell me the rest.'

Newman made Nicholas take off his coat and washed the blood from his face. While he was doing this, he told him everything about his uncle, Sir Mulberry Hawk and his sister. Nicholas listened in silence, then told Newman about his fight earlier that evening.

'I'm sure that was Sir Mulberry,' Newman said.

'Tomorrow morning, we must find another place for my mother to live,' Nicholas replied. 'Could you send Miss La Creevy to tell her? Please don't say anything about what happened tonight. I also want you to deliver a short letter to my uncle.'

Early the next morning, Nicholas went to see his sister at Mrs Wititterly's house. Brother and sister immediately fell into each other's arms.

'I've been so unhappy, dear brother,' Kate cried. 'Don't leave me here or I shall die of a broken heart.'

'I'll never leave you anywhere again,' Nicholas promised.

Apologising quickly to the Wititterlys, he hurried with his sister to their mother's house by the river.

'Miss La Creevy has told me everything,' Mrs Nickleby sighed when they arrived. 'But I still don't understand. Is Sir Mulberry such a bad man? Why don't you speak to your uncle? Perhaps there has been some mistake ...?'

'My dear mother,' Nicholas replied, 'the time for talking has gone. After the terrible things that he has done, you must throw him out of your life. We do not owe him anything except our scorn. You must leave this house at once. We can stay in our old place at Miss La Creevy's until I can make other arrangements.'

'Everything is ready for you,' Miss La Creevy said. 'You'll all be very welcome.'

'But I've just spent eighteen pence on painting the ceiling,' Mrs Nickleby complained, and started crying.

While Miss La Creevy looked after their mother, Nicholas and Kate carried the furniture into a waiting cart. After the three women had finally left, Nicholas hurried to meet Newman. He gave him a letter for his uncle and the key to the house.

'When you see my mother and sister at Miss La Creevy's, don't say anything about last night,' he reminded him.

Newman took the letter and key, and gave them to Ralph in his office.

'What's this?' Ralph said, picking up the key.

'It came with the letter. A boy brought them a quarter of an hour ago,' Newman lied.

Ralph opened the letter and read:

I know all about you and your evil plans. Your brother's widow and her daughter refuse any more of your help. They hate you as much as I do. I hope that on your death-bed you will feel ashamed of yourself.

Ralph Nickleby read the letter twice, then dropped it to the floor. He sat quietly at his desk, staring angrily at the wall. He did not notice the small smile on his old clerk's lips.

4.1 Were you right?

Look back at your answers to Activity 3.4. What are these people thinking?
Match the sentences on the right to the people.

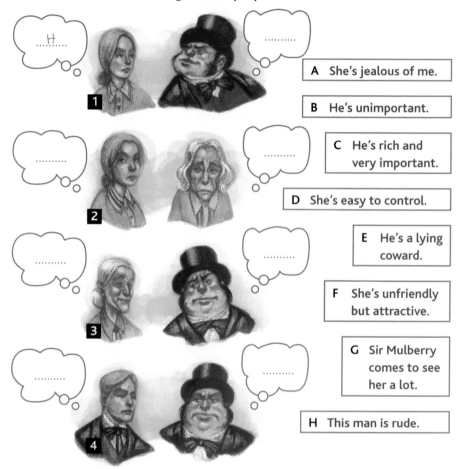

.....H.....

....

A She's jealous of me.

1

B He's unimportant.

....

....

C He's rich and very important.

D She's easy to control.

2

....

....

E He's a lying coward.

F She's unfriendly but attractive.

3

....

....

G Sir Mulberry comes to see her a lot.

H This man is rude.

4

4.2 What more did you learn?

Put these events in the right order, A–H.

1 ☐A☐ Kate finds another job.

2 ☐ Nicholas receives a letter.

3 ☐ Kate visits her uncle.

4 ☐ Mrs Nickleby meets Kate at the theatre.

5 ☐ Ralph receives an angry letter.

6 ☐ Mrs Nickleby and Kate leave their house.

7 ☐ Mrs Nickleby writes Kate a letter.

8 ☐ Nicholas has a fight.

4.3 **Language in use**

Look at the sentence on the right. Then finish these sentences with a verb from the box below. Use past perfect forms.

> She did not know that Newman **had received** a letter from Nicholas.

embarrass feel leave sit tell meet

A few weeks before starting her new job with the Wititterlys, Kate
1 ....*had met*.............. Sir Mulberry Hawk once at her uncle's house.
Unfortunately for Kate, this horrible old man 2 ....
next to her at dinner and 3 .... her all evening with his
rude jokes and wet-lipped smiles. She 4 .... so upset that
she 5 .... the table. After dinner, Sir Mulberry
6 .... her uncle that he wanted to meet her again.

4.4 **What's next?**

If you were Ralph Nickleby, what would you do next? Why? Discuss this with another student and make notes on a possible plan.

PLAN OF ACTION
....
....
....
....
....
....
....
....
....
....
....
....

CHAPTER 7

A Change of Luck

'But I am looking for work,' Nicholas replied.
'What?' the old man said with surprise.

Two days later, Ralph Nickleby learnt about Nicholas's attack on Sir Mulberry Hawk. He sat in his office and wondered what to do about the boy. While he was thinking, he received an unexpected visit from Wackford Squeers. Squeers had come to London to find more pupils for Dotheboys Hall, and he also wanted to talk to Ralph about his nephew. The two men sat together, planning their **revenge**.

Meanwhile, Mrs Nickleby and Kate were back in their old rooms in Miss La Creevy's house, and Nicholas decided to introduce them to Smike. Smike was shy at first, but Kate and Miss La Creevy were very kind to him. They soon persuaded Mrs Nickleby, who was unsure of him, to let him stay.

The next day, Nicholas returned to the job agency near Oxford Street. Before he went in, he looked at the advertisements in the window. While he was looking, an old gentleman in a blue coat and white hat walked towards the window and stood in the street next to him. Nicholas looked at him out of the corner of his eye.

revenge /rɪ'vendʒ/ (n) your punishment for someone who has harmed you
meanwhile /'miːnwaɪl/ (adv) while something else is happening

The old gentleman suddenly looked at Nicholas, and Nicholas looked away. 'I'm sorry,' he said, his face red with embarrassment. 'I didn't mean to be rude.'

'I'm not offended,' the man said with a smile.

There was something so friendly about the man's smile, his round face and the warm look in his eyes, that Nicholas spoke again.

'There are a lot of jobs here, sir,' he said, half-smiling.

'There are,' the man agreed. 'I feel so sorry for the people who have to come here.' He began to move away, but then noticed Nicholas's expression. 'You wanted to say something, young man?' he said.

'I was wondering why you were looking at these advertisements,' Nicholas replied.

'Did you think I was looking for work?' Nicholas shook his head. 'Ha! Ha!' laughed the old gentleman. 'A very natural thought, I suppose. I thought the same about you.'

'But I *am* looking for work,' Nicholas replied.

'What?' the old man said with surprise. 'A well-behaved, polite young gentleman like you? I don't believe it.'

Nicholas told him about the death of his father and the unhappy situation of his poor mother and sister. Before he realized it, he had told the kind old man almost everything about his life. He did not, however, say much about his uncle.

The old man listened with great attention. When Nicholas had finished his story, he said, 'Come along with me. We mustn't lose a minute.'

The old gentleman took Nicholas across London to a quiet square in East London, near the Bank of England, and led him into the oldest, cleanest-looking house in the square. The name *Cheeryble Brothers* was above the door.

Nicholas followed the old gentleman across a large, busy hall that was filled with boxes of cotton and other material. They went across a yard and into another building. Inside this building, which was the counting-house, an old, large-faced man with silver glasses was sitting at a desk.

'Is my brother in his room, Tim?' asked the old gentleman.

'Yes, he is, Mr Cheeryble,' replied the old clerk, looking at Nicholas over the top of his glasses.

Mr Cheeryble led Nicholas into another office. Nicholas couldn't believe his eyes when he saw Mr Cheeryble's brother – the two gentlemen looked exactly the same!

'Brother Ned, I'd like you to meet a young friend of mine who needs our help.'

'What does he need, Brother Charles?' the other man asked, looking at Nicholas with a kind smile.

Charles told his brother the details of Nicholas's situation and, after a long conversation, Ned went next door to speak to the old clerk, Tim Linkinwater. When he returned, he brought Tim Linkinwater with him.

'We've decided,' Ned told Nicholas, 'that you can work in the counting-house with Mr Linkinwater. Would you like that?'

Nicholas's eyes filled with tears of happiness. He did not know what to say.

'No, no, not a word now,' Charles said as Nicholas tried to thank him. 'You must return home. Your mother and sister will be worried about you. After we have checked a few details about you, Tim Linkinwater will visit you tonight.'

Nicholas returned home and told everybody his good news. That evening, Tim Linkinwater arrived and invited Nicholas to start work the next morning.

'The brothers will pay you 120 pounds a year,' Tim informed him. 'In addition to this, you and your family are welcome to move into a small **cottage** that belongs to them. It's not far from the office, the rent is very low, and they will also lend you the money to buy furniture.'

One week later, Mrs Nickleby, Kate, Smike and Nicholas moved into their new home.

Meanwhile, several miles away, Ralph Nickleby was still busy planning his revenge.

cottage /ˈkɒtɪdʒ/ (n) a small house

CHAPTER 8

Kidnap

*As Smike was crossing the corner of a side-street, he felt
a hand on his collar.*

While Mrs Nickleby, Kate and Miss La Creevy were busy decorating the cottage and Nicholas was busy in his new job, Smike spent all his time working in the garden. As the garden filled with flowers, his heart filled with happiness.

'You've made the garden a place of great beauty, Smike,' Kate told him one evening, standing next him and looking at the flowers. 'We're all so happy to see *you* so happy.'

Mrs Nickleby also saw how enthusiastically he worked and how much pleasure the garden gave him. She became very fond of him, too, and soon everybody was treating him as a member of the family. Smike had never felt so happy.

One evening, he was walking back to the cottage in East London from Miss La Creevy's house. As he was crossing the corner of a side-street, he felt a hand on his collar. Then he was pulled backwards and pushed against a wall.

'Well, what a surprise!' said Wackford Squeers, looking at Smike with his one eye. Then he turned to his son, who was jumping up and down with excitement next to him. 'Wackford, my boy, go and find a coach.'

Smike fought and kicked as hard as he could, but he was too weak to escape. Soon a coach arrived and Squeers pushed Smike inside. He sat down opposite the frightened boy and stared at him with an unpleasant smile. Then, with a loud laugh, he hit Smike several times across the face.

'It isn't a dream!' he laughed. 'It's real. You thought that you could escape me, didn't you? Well, you were wrong!'

'Let me go home!' Smike cried, looking wildly around.

'You *are* going home!' Squeers replied, hitting him again. 'You'll soon be back at Dotheboys Hall, where you belong.'

After a long journey, the coach stopped outside a small house with green windows. Squeers pulled Smike out of the coach, paid the driver and pushed Smike into the house.

In the front room, a fat man was having dinner with his wife. His name was Snawley, and he had sent his two sons to Dotheboys Hall. When he had invited Squeers and his son to stay at his house while they were in London, Squeers had accepted immediately – it was much cheaper than staying at the Saracen's Head!

'Here's the boy that ran away and stole my wife's ring,' Squeers told the surprised couple. 'The ungrateful little animal! If there wasn't a lady here, I would hit him!'

'Where has he been staying?' Mr Snawley asked.

'Probably with that man Nickleby. Is that right, Smike?'

Smike refused to answer, so Squeers pushed him upstairs into a small room. He took the boy's shoes and coat and locked him inside.

The next morning, Squeers was having breakfast at the Saracen's Head with his son when three people walked into the coffee-room. His daughter, Fanny, with her friend Tilda and Tilda's new husband, John Browdie, had just arrived from Yorkshire for a short holiday in London. While they were all having breakfast, Squeers told them about Smike.

'Poor boy,' John Browdie said when Squeers had finished his story. 'Where are you keeping him?'

'On the top floor of my lodgings,' Squeers replied.

John Browdie laughed loudly and shook the schoolmaster's hand. 'The cleverest schoolmaster in all England!' he said. 'Congratulations!'

'Thank you,' Squeers said, pulling his hand away. 'It's lucky you came today. We're travelling back to Yorkshire tomorrow morning. If you don't come for tea with me this evening, you won't see us again in London.'

'We'll be at your lodgings at six o'clock tonight,' John Browdie promised.

Squeers gave the farmer Mr Snawley's address, then left with his son.

That evening, John Browdie, Tilda and Fanny arrived at Snawley's house at six o'clock exactly. John seemed strangely quiet while they were having tea in the front room.

After a short time he said, 'I don't feel very well. It's probably the long journey and all the excitement. I think I need to lie down for half an hour.'

Tilda helped him upstairs into Squeers's bedroom. John closed his eyes, and Tilda returned downstairs.

'He's sleeping like a baby,' she told the others.

In fact, John Browdie was not sleeping at all. When his wife had gone downstairs, he got off the bed, took off his shoes and softly left the room. The key to the room next to his was still in the door. Quietly turning it, he opened the door and hurried inside, where Smike was lying quietly on the bed under a thin blanket.

'Don't be afraid,' John whispered, putting his big hand gently over Smike's mouth. 'I'm here to help you escape.'

Not knowing who this big stranger was, and shaking with fear, Smike went with the farmer into the next bedroom, where he found his coat and shoes on a chair. He put them on and followed the big man quietly down the stairs. He felt even more frightened when he heard Squeers and the others talking in the front room.

'Don't worry,' John whispered when they reached the bottom of the stairs. 'I'll make sure that no one follows you.' He opened the front door quietly. 'Quickly! Go now!'

Smike gave Browdie a confused but grateful look, and ran off into the darkness.

A few hours later, he arrived at Newman Noggs's lodgings and, after a hot drink, told him his story.

'You're tired,' Noggs said, when Smike had finished talking. 'You must stay here for the night. I'll tell the others that you're back. They've been worried about you all day.'

But Smike refused to be left alone and walked with Noggs through the dark, empty streets of London. They arrived at the Nickleby's cottage just as it was getting light.

Everybody was relieved to see him. There was much congratulation and noisy conversation, and Smike cried with happiness to be safely back with his 'family' again.

5.1 Were you right?

Look back at your answers to Activity 4.4. Then read these sentences. Only one of them is true. Which one? Correct the others.

1 Ralph invites Squeers to London to help him with his revenge.

   ....

2 Smike works in the kitchen of the new house.

   ....

3 The Cheeryble brothers offer the Nicklebys a free home and furniture.

   ....

4 Squeers plans to take Smike back to Dotheboys Hall.

   ....

5 John Browdie feels ill after his long journey.

   ....

5.2 What more did you learn?

Whose thoughts might these be? Who are they thinking about?

1 'Why is that old gentleman looking in this window?'
   ....Nicholas......... is thinking about ....

2 'Why is this well-dressed gentleman looking for a job?'
   .... is thinking about ....

3 'He's made the garden beautiful.'
   .... is thinking about ....

4 'I'll take him back to Yorkshire.'
   .... is thinking about ....

5 'I don't know who you are, but thank you.'
   .... is thinking about ....

6 'How did he escape?'
   .... is thinking about ....

3 Language in use

Look at the sentence on the right. Then rewrite these sentences using passive verb forms. Include the 'doer' if that information is important.

> Smike **was pulled** backwards **and pulled** against the wall (**by** Squeers).

1 Squeers visited Ralph Nickleby.

Ralph Nickleby .... *was visited by Squeers* ....

2 Nicholas did not offend the old gentleman.

The old gentleman ....

3 The old gentleman took Nicholas across London.

Nicholas ....

4 'The brothers will pay £120 a year.'

'You ....'

5 'You've made the garden a place of great beauty.'

'The garden ....'

6 'This boy stole my wife's ring.'

'My wife's ring ....'

4 What's next?

In the next chapter, Nicholas falls in love. Will there be any problems? Imagine what these people will think.

Kate	Ralph	Smike	the girl's father
....	....	....	....
....	....	....	....
....	....	....	....

CHAPTER 9

Love and War

'But I have a secret that will interest you.'
'Tell the world about it. I don't care.'

Later that morning, in the counting-house, Nicholas found it difficult to work. He was thinking about how to punish Wackford Squeers for kidnapping Smike. He was sure that his uncle had planned it. He was still thinking about this when he opened the door into Charles Cheeryble's office.

There, he saw a young lady on her knees at Mr Cheeryble's feet. It was the same girl that he had seen on his first visit to the job agency! Nicholas was so filled with surprise and affected by the girl's beauty that he could not move or speak. All thoughts of revenge against his uncle and Squeers disappeared from his mind. There were tears in the girl's eyes as she repeatedly thanked Mr Cheeryble for his kindness. Mr Cheeryble looked embarrassed and was asking her to rise.

Nicholas quietly left the room before the girl could see him. Later that morning, he asked Tim Linkinwater about the young lady in Mr Cheeryble's office, but the old clerk pretended not to hear.

Nicholas waited for the mysterious young lady's next visit, but days passed and there was no sign of her. Then, one day, he was sent out on some unusual business. He was sure that the young lady was visiting the office while he was away. This happened several times. Why, Nicholas thought, was everybody so unwilling to talk about her?

As the days passed, Nicholas could think of nothing except the beautiful young lady. Soon, he realised that he had fallen in love. He *had* to find out more information about her! Eventually, he could not keep the secret to himself. He told Newman Noggs about her and Newman promised to help.

'The next time you're sent away on business,' he said, 'I'll wait outside the building. When she leaves, I'll follow her home. Then I can tell you where she lives.'

Two days later, Nicholas was sent out on another piece of strange business. That evening, he returned excitedly and asked Newman for news. Unfortunately, Newman could not help him. He had followed the wrong girl!

◆

One evening, Ralph Nickleby was walking near St James's Park, on his way home. Although he had collected a lot of money for his business that day, he was in a bad mood. His heart was still poisoned with anger for his nephew, and he was still thinking of revenge. Sir Mulberry Hawk could not help him. He had been so badly hurt and publicly embarrassed after his fight with Nicholas that he had left London as soon as possible. Squeers had returned to Yorkshire, but that was no problem. He was thinking of a plan, and Squeers was going to help him succeed!

While he was walking it began to rain, so Ralph stood under a tree, still lost in thought. Suddenly, he noticed a man standing next to him. He was the same age as he was, but wore dirty, old clothes, and had a thin, hungry face. His skin was sunburnt, and his hair was pure white.

'You don't remember me, do you?' the man said.

Ralph stared at him. Then he stepped back in shock. Yes, he remembered the man. His name was Brooker. He had known him for a long time, but he had not seen him for eight years.

'I used to be your friend,' Brooker reminded him. 'I'm hungry. I only need a little bread …'

'Is this the way that you usually beg for money?' Ralph coldly replied.

'Yesterday was my first day back in London,' the old man continued. 'I've been looking for you. I'm nearly sixty years old and I have nothing in the world.'

'I'm sixty years old, too,' Ralph said. 'But I don't beg people for bread. I work and earn money for it.'

'I used to bring you good business, but you never thanked me. When I asked you for more money, you refused. Instead, you told the police about my debts and I was sent away on a prison ship for eight years. What help will you give me now?'

'None.'

'But I have a secret that will interest you.'

'Tell the world about it. I don't care. I'm not giving you any help. Now go away, or I shall make sure you go to prison again. And this time you'll never get out.'

With those words, Ralph walked off into the rain. Brooker stared at his back, his eyes filled with hate.

◆

At the end of their holiday in London, John Browdie and Tilda were having tea at the Nicklebys' cottage. While everybody was laughing and joking, there was a loud knock on the door and Ralph Nickleby walked in, followed by Wackford Squeers and Mr Snawley.

'Listen to what I have to say,' he told them. John Browdie and Nicholas stood up angrily, but Ralph looked straight past them at Mrs Nickleby. 'I shall talk to you, ma'am,' he said. 'I know that your mad son will refuse to listen to me. I am here to return a child to his parent.' He pointed at Smike, who was shaking with fear behind Nicholas's back. 'I have brought that boy's father here with me tonight.'

'My son!' cried Mr Snawley, hurrying past Nicholas and taking Smike in his arms. 'I've found you at last!'

'This is the boy's father,' Ralph said, pointing at Snawley, 'and here are the documents that prove it.'

He left the documents on the table for Nicholas and John Browdie to study.

'Dear Nicholas,' Kate said at last, looking over her brother's shoulder, 'is it true?'

'I'm afraid it is,' Nicholas replied quietly.

'Good!' said Squeers. 'So he's coming with us. There's a coach waiting outside, and the horses are getting cold.'

'No!' cried Smike, pulling away from Snawley. 'I'm not leaving!'

Squeers moved forwards, but John Browdie pushed him away and he fell to the floor. After a lot of loud argument and angry shouting, Nicholas picked Squeers up by the collar and threw him out of the door.

'I want my son,' Snawley demanded.

'Your son wants to stay here,' Nicholas replied. 'And I will not let him go back to that school!'

Snawley left the room, but Ralph stayed behind. He stared at Nicholas angrily. 'Mr Snawley is the boy's father,' he said, 'and he will have him.'

CHAPTER 10

Madeline Bray

*Nicholas left the room and went down the stairs, his heart
filled with happiness. He had found his love at last!*

T he next day, Nicholas told Charles Cheeryble everything that had happened.
Charles listened carefully.

'Your story does not surprise me,' he said. 'Your uncle visited us this morning.
He came here to complain about you, to poison our ears with lies. But we refused
to listen and made him leave.'

'How can I ever thank you?' Nicholas said, relieved that he had such good
friends.

'By saying nothing more about the subject,' Charles replied. 'Don't worry. We
shall protect you and your family. But now I have a job for you. It's a special job.
You accidentally saw a young lady in my office some time ago. Or perhaps you
have forgotten …'

'Oh no, sir,' Nicholas said, a feeling of great excitement rising inside him. 'I
remember it very well.'

'Her mother was a very beautiful woman,' Charles said. 'I was in love with
her, but she married another man. Their life was not happy. They had a daughter
– the girl you saw in my office – but they had no money. Twelve months before
her death, the mother came to me for help. I gave her money, which her husband
wasted. When she died, she was a sad, heart-broken woman.

'Her husband is still alive. He owes money to a lot of people, and he lives in
a secret place to hide from them. His daughter worked for two long years to give
him money, but eventually she needed help. She came to me because I had been
a friend of her mother's, and I offered to help her. But she only accepted a very
small amount of money. I wanted to help her more, but she refused. Her father is
still alive and he hates me. He knows that his wife really wanted to marry me. If
he knew the money came from me, he would waste it all. Madeline comes to me
secretly, usually by night, but only accepts the smallest amount of money. This
situation cannot continue, Nicholas, and I want you to help me.'

'I'd be glad to,' Nicholas said. 'What do you want me to do?'

'She's a wonderful artist, but she doesn't sell anything. You can visit her and
pay for some paintings. Madeline will know that Ned and I have sent you,
but her father will not know that you have not ordered any. You will pay a
good price and her father will not know that the money comes from Ned and
myself.'

Nicholas, of course, agreed to help at once.

The young lady and her father (whose name was Bray) lived in a cheap, dirty house near the prison. Nicholas knocked on the door nervously, and was shown upstairs. Although there was not much furniture, the small room was filled with flowers and paintings. And at a little table by the window sat the young lady of Nicholas's dreams! She was quietly painting, and seemed to Nicholas more beautiful than ever.

In a chair by the empty fireplace sat her father – a sick man in his fifties who looked much older.

'Madeline, who is this?' Mr Bray said. 'Who said that strangers could visit us here?'

'I've come to pay for some paintings that your daughter did for me, Mr Bray,' Nicholas said, placing an envelope on the table in front of the girl.

'Check the money, Madeline,' Mr Bray said.

'I'm sure the money's correct, Father,' Madeline said softly.

'If that's true, ring the bell. Tell the servant to get me a newspaper, some fresh fruit and a bottle of wine!'

'I also want to order something else,' Nicholas said. 'Perhaps a picture of the trees in the park? Don't worry about the time or cost. When would you like me to call again?'

'Three or four weeks,' Madeline replied, looking at Nicholas shyly.

'No – sooner!' her father said. 'We'll need more money before then!'

Nicholas left the room and went down the stairs, his heart filled with happiness. He had found his love at last!

◆

Meanwhile, several miles away, Ralph was talking to a man in his office. Arthur Gride was also a moneylender. He was an ugly old man of about seventy-five years old, with a pointed chin, toothless mouth and unhealthy yellow skin. But this did not stop him from talking about love!

'I'm a lucky man,' said Arthur Gride. 'I'm going to get married.'

'You? Who would want to marry *you*?' Ralph smiled scornfully. 'A toothless old woman as ugly as yourself?'

'No,' Arthur said. 'She's a beautiful young girl with dark eyes, and lovely red lips – and she's only eighteen years old!'

'What's her name?' Ralph asked, staring at Gride coldly.

'Do you remember Walter Bray? We both did business with him, and he owes us both money. I've visited him several times over the last six months. He owes me 1700 pounds.'

'And he owes me over 900 pounds,' Ralph said. 'But why are you telling me about him now?'

'Well, I'm going to marry his daughter, Madeline. I haven't asked her father yet, but he'll agree. If he lets me marry his daughter, I'll forget his debts. I'll even give him some money and a place to live across the river. I've talked to his doctor, and he won't live long. He's certain to agree to my request, don't you think? His daughter will have to obey him, but I need your help.'

'How?'

'I'm a shy, nervous man. I need you to talk to the father for me. You're good with words. He'll listen to you.'

'There's something more, isn't there?' Ralph said, narrowing his eyes and studying Arthur's ugly old face.

'No, no ...'

'Don't lie. I know you. You're as greedy as I am. If you don't tell me everything, I won't help you.'

'Well, there's a little house that belongs to this girl. Nobody knows about it – not even her. If I marry her, the house will be mine.'

'All right,' Ralph said, smiling thoughtfully. 'I agree to help you. But you must promise to pay me all of the money that Bray owes me. I also want an extra 500 pounds.'

After much complaining, Gride unwillingly agreed. The two men left immediately to visit Walter Bray and, after half an hour of listening to Ralph, Bray agreed to his daughter's marriage one week later.

◆

Life for the Nicklebys in their cottage was good. The Cheeryble brothers visited them often. Sometimes, they brought with them their nephew, Frank, who had just returned from abroad. They spent many happy evenings together.

Although Nicholas was happy, too, he was worried about Smike. The boy had recently become much quieter. He also seemed to be growing weaker, and spent more time alone in his room. However, the doctor told Nicholas not to worry. The kidnap had been a bad experience for Smike, and he needed time to forget it.

One night, while Frank Cheeryble was telling Mrs Nickleby and Kate about his adventures abroad, Nicholas went up to Smike's room. The boy was lying quietly in his bed.

'What's the matter?' Nicholas asked softly. 'Are you feeling ill?'

'No, I'm all right,' Smike replied.

'But you seem so sad. Won't you tell me why?'

'I can't. Not now. I hate myself for being like this. You're all so good and kind to me. But my heart is full. You don't know how full it is. One day, I'll tell you the reason.'

CHAPTER 11

An Evil Marriage

*'No gentleman would make his daughter do what you
are making your daughter do.'*

Nicholas met Newman Noggs for a drink and Noggs gave him news about his uncle. A strange man called Brooker kept coming to the office, but Ralph refused to meet him. Nicholas then told Noggs about his job, and about the beautiful girl with the sick father. When he told him her name, Newman jumped up from his chair.

'Oh, no!' he cried. 'How can you do nothing and let this terrible marriage happen?'

'What do you mean?' Nicholas said, confused by his friend's strange behaviour.

'Haven't you heard?' Newman said, his eyes moving around wildly. 'Tomorrow she's going to marry a horrible old moneylender called Arthur Gride – a man worse than your uncle, if that's possible. Your uncle has arranged it all. I heard them discussing it in his office last week.'

Nicholas stood up and forced Newman down into his chair. 'Tell me everything!' he demanded.

Newman told him the details of what he had heard. When he had finished, a wild look came into Nicholas's eyes.

'What are you going to do?' Newman asked, frightened.

'What *can* I do?' Nicholas replied, his face pale with anger. 'The brothers are out of town on business. If I visit my uncle, I'll only make things worse. No, I must go and see Madeline immediately and tell her of my true feelings for her. When her father sees how much I love his daughter, perhaps he'll change his mind. It's my only hope!'

Before Newman could say anything to stop him, Nicholas ran out into the street.

When he arrived at their lodgings, Madeline and her father were sitting in their room. Nicholas had not seen Madeline for three weeks, and he was shocked by the terrible paleness of her face and the dark shadows under her lovely eyes.

The room had changed, too. There were no paintings on the walls or flowers on the table.

'What do you want?' Bray said from his chair by the fire. 'Be quick, because my daughter and I have important things to think about.'

'There's something that I need to discuss with your daughter in private, sir,' Nicholas said politely, hiding his anger with difficulty.

'We don't need your business any more,' Bray replied rudely. 'So you can leave, unless you have something else to say?'

'Only this,' Nicholas said, unable to control his anger any more. 'I thought you were a gentleman, sir, but I was wrong. No gentleman would make his daughter do what you are making your daughter do.'

'You can't talk to me like that!' Bray said angrily. 'You're only an ordinary shop-boy!'

He tried to stand up, but his anger had made him weak. He fell back in his chair and closed his eyes. Nicholas took Madeline's arm and led her quietly out of the room.

'If you have more business for me,' Madeline said anxiously when they were outside the room, 'please leave it until the day after tomorrow.'

'That will be too late,' Nicholas replied.

Madeline tried to walk away, but Nicholas gently stopped her.

'Please listen to me,' he said.

She stared at him quietly as he tried to persuade her not to marry Arthur Gride. 'I have no choice,' she explained. 'It is my duty to my father.'

He tried again, but she refused to listen and she went back into the room to be with her father.

Nicholas returned home, his heart aching with unhappiness.

That evening, he visited Arthur Gride. He told the old moneylender that Madeline Bray hated him. 'If you were a gentleman, you would think about the pain in that innocent girl's heart,' Nicholas said.

Gride listened to him in scornful silence, then said, 'I understand you better than you think. You want her for yourself, don't you? But you can't have her! She's my lovely little wife. Do you think she'll cry for you? I hope so, because she looks prettier in tears.'

'You evil old man,' Nicholas said, his face red with anger.

Without warning, Arthur Gride ran across the room and put his head out of the window. 'Help! Help!' he shouted into the street. 'Thief! Robber!'

Nicholas was so angry that he almost attacked Arthur Gride.

Instead, he turned quickly and left the room.

◆

The next morning, Arthur Gride got up early and put on his best suit. He spoke to his half-deaf old **housekeeper**, Peg Sliderskew, about the arrangements for food, and then he went to Ralph Nickleby's house.

housekeeper /ˈhaʊsˌkiːpə/ (n) someone who is paid to cook and clean in a house

Ralph laughed when he heard about his nephew's visit the night before.

'Good!' he thought. 'I'm getting revenge on him at last!'

The two men hired a coach and went to Walter Bray's lodgings.

'Where's the lucky girl?' Ralph asked Bray as soon as he and Gride had entered the room.

'She was very ill last night,' Bray explained. 'She's crying in her room. But don't worry; she'll be better in a minute. It's only a girl's usual nervousness just before her wedding.'

'She won't delay us, will she?' Ralph asked.

'No, I've been talking to her all morning. She'll be down in a minute,' Bray replied.

Arthur Gride sat in a corner of the room and played impatiently with the buttons of his coat.

Bray looked at him scornfully. 'Look at that man,' he whispered to Ralph. 'This marriage is a cruel thing to do to an innocent young girl, don't you think?'

'No,' Ralph replied coldly, surprised by Bray's sudden pity for his daughter. 'It would be more cruel if he were younger. He's an old man. He'll die soon, and Miss Madeline will become a rich young widow.'

'That's true,' Bray said thoughtfully, but he still did not look happy. 'I'll go upstairs to finish dressing,' he said. 'When I come down, I'll bring Madeline with me.'

When he had left the room, Ralph turned to Gride. 'He looks very ill,' he said. 'If he doesn't die soon, I'll be very surprised.'

Gride laughed quietly, but did not reply.

The two men sat waiting in silence. After a short time, they heard footsteps outside the door – but it was not Bray and his daughter. It was Nicholas and his sister, Kate!

Ralph stood up, his face pale with anger. Gride took Ralph's arm, his eyes filled with fear.

'What do you want?' Ralph demanded.

'I've come here to save Madeline from this evil marriage,' Nicholas replied.

'Leave the room, girl,' Ralph told Kate. 'I advise you not to see what I'm going to do to your brother.'

'I will not go,' Kate said, standing proudly by her brother. 'I'm going to speak to the girl and her father. Perhaps they will listen to me.'

'I know how jealous your brother is,' Arthur Gride said from behind Ralph's back. 'But it's too late! The girl is mine!'

Suddenly, there was a loud scream from the room above them. Nicholas ran upstairs and saw a crowd of neighbours already in the bedroom.

'What's happened?' Nicholas asked.

'It's Mr Bray,' replied an old woman. 'He's dead.'

Nicholas pushed through the crowd and saw Bray lying on the floor.
Madeline was lying with her head on his shoulder, crying. Nicholas gently took
her arm and led her from the room.

'I'm the young girl's nearest friend,' he informed the watching crowd of
neighbours. 'My sister and I will take care of her until she is well.'

Nobody tried to stop him as he led Madeline, who was too upset and shocked
to refuse, down the stairs and into the street.

As Kate ran across the road to hire a coach, Ralph called from the doorway,
'Leave the girl here!'

'I warn you,' Nicholas shouted back at his uncle, 'that your evil world is finished!'
With those words, he helped Madeline into the coach which Kate had found.

Ralph angrily watched the coach disappear around a corner, then unwillingly
agreed to go back to Gride's house. When they arrived, Gride knocked on the
door, but there was no answer.

'What's the matter?' Ralph said impatiently. 'Why doesn't anyone answer?'
'It's Peg, my housekeeper,' Gride explained. 'She's deaf.'

He knocked more loudly until the whole street could hear him, but still no one answered the door. Finally, the two moneylenders climbed over a fence into Gride's back yard. The house was dark and empty.

The two men looked in every room, but there was no sign of Peg. Then Gride fell on his knees beside a large box and screamed like an animal in pain.

'I've been robbed!' he cried.

'Robbed? Of money?' Ralph wanted to know.

'No, worse than money! Worse than money!' Gride shouted, throwing papers around the room. 'It's my business papers with all my secret information. She saw me reading them last night. She'll show them to someone and they'll take all my money. She's destroyed me!'

'Calm down!' Ralph said, shaking Gride roughly. 'She probably isn't far away. I'll call the police …'

'No!' Gride shouted, even more frightened than before. 'If the police see my papers, I'll go to prison!'

Eventually, when Gride had calmed down, Ralph went home.

A short time later, he sent Newman Noggs with a letter to the Saracen's Head. 'If Mr Squeers is there,' he told Newman, 'tell him to see me at once.'

When Squeers arrived, Ralph told him how his nephew had ruined Arthur Gride's wedding to Madeline Bray. 'If my nephew marries her, he'll become a very rich man,' he said. 'And that will make him a very dangerous enemy.'

'How will he become rich?'

'It seems that Madeline owns a house. She doesn't know it, but there are secret documents to prove it. Arthur Gride had the papers, but his housekeeper has stolen them. I want you to find this woman, and bring the papers to me. If I can destroy them, my nephew will never get the money. I'll pay you fifty pounds as soon as I have those papers.'

Squeers listened to this with greedy ears, his one eye and his mouth wide open. 'But how do I know where to find her?' he asked.

'Don't worry about that. People have tried to hide from me before, but I've always found them. When I know where she is, I'll tell you. Your part of the job will be easy. You will become her friend. Then you can discover where she has hidden the papers.'

Squeers thought for a moment, then said, 'I'll do it for a hundred pounds.'

Ralph agreed immediately.

6.1 Where you right?

Look back at your answers to Activity 5.4. Then answer the questions.

1 Who is happy about Nicholas's love for Madeline?

....

2 Who is not happy about it?

....

6.2 What more did you learn?

Complete the sentences with words from Box A and words from Box B.

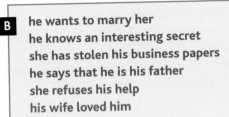

A	**B**
Arthur Gride	he wants to marry her
Charles Cheeryble	he knows an interesting secret
Brooker	she has stolen his business papers
Mr Snawley	he says that he is his father
Madeline	she refuses his help
Peg Sliderskew	his wife loved him

1 Ralph has a problem with (A) .... because

(B) ....

2 Smike is afraid of (A) .... because

(B) ....

3 Charles Cheeryble is worried about (A) .... because

(B) ....

4 Mr Bray hates (A) .... because

(B) ....

5 Madeline is afraid of (A) .... because

(B) ....

6 Arthur Gride is angry with (A) .... because

(B) ....

3 Language in use

Look at the sentence on the right. Then change the words in *italics* to a word from the story that has the same meaning. The first letter has been given to you.

> She **repeatedly** thanked Mr Cheeryble for his kindness.

1 Sir Mulberry had been .p.............................. embarrassed [*in public*].

2 Nicholas .a.............................. saw a young lady in Mr Cheeryble's office [*by accident*].

3 Bray's daughter asked Mr Cheeryble for help [*in the end*] .e.............................. .

4 Nicholas [*was nervous when he*] .n.............................. knocked on the door.

5 Ralph smiled at Arthur Gride [*with scorn*] .s.............................. .

6 [*In the end*] .f.............................. the moneylenders climbed over the fence.

4 What's next?

Look at the pictures in the last three chapters. Whose story will have a happy ending? Whose will have a sad ending? Make two lists.

happy ending	sad ending

CHAPTER 12

Poor Smike

'I saw him – over there, behind the trees! It was the man who took me to that horrible school, years ago!'

Madeline was now living with the Nicklebys in their cottage, but the shock of her father's death had made her very ill. While she stayed in bed, Kate took care of her, and by the time Madeline's health improved she and Kate had become good friends.

These were proud times for Mrs Nickleby. She noticed that Frank Cheeryble often came to the cottage with Nicholas after work. She was sure that he was interested in Kate, and began to dream of a wonderful wedding for her daughter!

When she told Nicholas about Frank's interest in Kate, Nicholas was surprised, but he was also secretly relieved. He had been afraid that Frank was also in love in Madeline. He liked Frank a lot, and he was glad that they would not have to become enemies.

However, Nicholas became increasingly worried about Smike, who had become very ill. The doctor told him that Smike's condition was serious and he advised him to take the boy away from London as soon as possible. The fresh country air might cure him. So Nicholas took Smike to Devon, in southwest England, where he had lived as a child.

◆

Meanwhile, Ralph Nickleby had discovered where Peg Sliderskew, Gride's housekeeper, was living. She was in an upper room in a dirty old house near Lambeth, in southeast London. Ralph informed Squeers, who moved into an empty room in the same house and soon became friendly with her. One evening, he took a bottle of strong alcohol into her room and sat talking to her by the fire.

After the old woman had drunk a few glasses, Squeers told her how Arthur Gride's wedding plans were ruined. Peg Sliderskew laughed so much that she nearly fell out of her chair.

'I'm glad,' she said. 'Gride's a horrible, greedy old man. He treated me very badly. That's why I ran away with his papers.'

'I'll be happy to help with Gride's papers,' Squeers suggested, when Peg was completely drunk. 'I can tell you which ones to keep and which ones to burn.'

The old woman walked with a drunken smile to a cupboard. She took the papers out of a box and spread them out on the floor by the fire. Squeers was so busy studying them that he did not hear the door opening behind him. He did not see Frank Cheeryble and Newman Noggs walking quietly into the room.

Eventually, he found the paper that he wanted. 'Madeline Bray!' he said excitedly, putting it in his coat pocket.

'What did you say?' Peg asked, turning her head.

She saw the two men, but it was too late to save Squeers. Newman Noggs lifted his arm and brought a thick stick down heavily onto his head. The old schoolmaster's one eye opened wide with surprise, then he fell forwards across the floor.

After a two-day journey to Devon, Nicholas rented a small farmhouse. At first, Smike was strong enough to go for short walks in the surrounding fields. Nicholas also hired a horse and cart and drove Smike around the countryside. He showed the boy the house where he had lived, and he even found a rose-tree in the garden that his little sister Kate had planted.

However, as Smike grew weaker, travelling became impossible. On sunny days, Nicholas sat outside with him under some apple trees. One evening, they were watching the sun go down behind the hills. It was so warm that Nicholas fell asleep. Suddenly, he was woken by a scream.

'What is it?' he asked anxiously.

'I saw him – over there, behind the trees! It was the man who took me to that horrible school, years ago!'

Nicholas searched among the trees, but there was no one there. 'You were dreaming,' he said when he returned.

'No, I wasn't dreaming,' Smike replied, holding tightly onto Nicholas's arm. 'Promise me you'll never leave me! Promise!'

Over the next few days, Smike became much weaker. Nicholas saw now that there was no hope for his young friend. A life of suffering and pain had made him too weak to fight his illness.

One fine, autumn day, Nicholas sat by Smike's bedside. Smike was lying with his eyes closed, breathing gently. Suddenly, he opened his eyes. There was a small smile on his pale face.

'I've had such pleasant dreams,' he said softly.

'What about?' Nicholas asked.

The dying boy turned towards him and hugged his neck. 'I shall soon be there.' There was a short silence, then Smike spoke again. 'I'm not afraid to die,' he said. 'But first I must tell you something. You've been so good to me, and I can't keep any secrets from you. You asked me once why I had changed. Do you remember? You wondered why I spent so much time alone. Shall I tell you why?'

'Not if it makes you unhappy.'

Smike explained that he had been in love with Nicholas's sister. 'I've been so unhappy,' he said. 'I'm so sorry. Will you ever forgive me?'

Nicholas went on his knees by Smike's bed and held his hand. 'Oh, you poor boy,' he said with tears in his eyes. 'Of course I forgive you.'

'Now,' Smike said softly, 'I am happy.'

He died later that night, quietly, in his sleep.

CHAPTER 13

Ralph's Final Defeat

*What good was all his money now? He had murdered
his own child.*

R alph sat alone in his room and stared at his untouched breakfast. He had a strange feeling that something was wrong. It was nearly midday, and Newman Noggs had still not come to work. He sent his housekeeper to Noggs's home to find him.

'He's not there,' she informed him when she returned. 'He hasn't been home all night, and no one knows where he is. But there's a gentleman waiting for you downstairs.'

Ralph went downstairs, where Charles Cheeryble was waiting to speak to him. Ralph refused to speak to him, and sent him away at once. Then he put on his hat and coat and went to visit Snawley. But Snawley's wife angrily refused to let him see her husband.

'He's in so much trouble because of you!' she said, and shut the door in his face.

Next, Ralph went to the Saracen's Head for news about Squeers, but nobody had seen him for ten days. He decided to visit the house in Lambeth where Squeers and Peg Sliderskew were staying, but he found the two rooms empty. He eventually discovered from a neighbour that a one-eyed man and a drunken old woman had been carried away from the building by two men the night before.

'They've been caught by the police,' Ralph thought. 'I must tell Arthur Gride at once.'

Arthur Gride, however, did not want to speak to him. 'Go away,' he called from an upstairs window. 'It isn't safe.'

'Come down and open the door,' Ralph demanded, but without success. Gride closed the upstairs window, and there was silence inside the house.

'This is mad!' Ralph said to himself. 'Nobody wants to talk to me. I must find out what's happening.'

Unwillingly, he decided to visit the Cheeryble brothers.

'Which of you visited me this morning?' Ralph asked, looking from one man to the other, unable to tell the difference.

'It was my brother,' said brother Ned.

Without waiting for an invitation, Ralph sat down and crossed his legs. 'Now, gentlemen, what do you wish to say?'

Ned rang a bell and Newman Noggs walked into the room.

'What are *you* doing here?' Ralph asked with a scornful smile.

'I'm here because I hate the cruel way that you treat honest people,' Noggs replied. 'You enjoy making innocent people suffer. I've seen how you've treated your own family. I've seen you lie about Smike's father and persuade a selfish father to sell his daughter to Arthur Gride. I've seen it all.'

'You can't prove any of this,' Ralph said, still smiling.

'Yes, we can,' brother Charles said. 'Last night, the man Snawley told us everything.' The smile went from Ralph's face. 'Mr Noggs came to us for help a few weeks ago,' Charles explained. 'He had been spying on you for a long time, and had heard all your conversations with Snawley, Gride and Squeers. We quickly discovered that Snawley was not Smike's real father. He told us that the whole lie had been your idea. Last night, Mr Noggs and my nephew found your friend Squeers with the stolen papers in his pocket. You were trying to stop Madeline Bray getting the house that belonged to her, weren't you? Well, your friend Squeers is already with the police.'

'If all this is true,' said Ralph, 'why am I not in prison with him?'

'We wanted to help you,' brother Ned said. 'We have told you all this before telling the police about you. We have given you the chance to leave London.'

Ralph smiled scornfully. 'I don't believe a word that you say. I shall not leave London. You have not heard the last of me!' With these proud words, he left the room.

He went straight to the police station, where he found Squeers sitting in a prison room.

'What happened last night?' Ralph asked him.

Squeers explained everything, his one eye filled with hate as he spoke. 'It's all your fault,' the schoolmaster said angrily. 'Why didn't you let me burn the papers? Now the police have them. Madeline Bray will get her house, and my life is ruined because of you.'

'The police can't do anything,' Ralph said. 'We'll invent a story, and ...'

But Squeers refused to listen. 'No,' he said. 'I'm finished with you. I'm going to tell the police everything.'

Ralph left Squeers and angrily walked home. He sat down in the dark, put his head in his hands and did not move for an hour.

At ten o'clock there was a knock on the door. It was Tim Linkinwater.

'Mr Nickleby,' Tim said. 'Something important has happened. You must come with me at once.'

'Why should I? For a repeat performance of this morning?'

'No,' replied Tim. 'It's bad news for you, I'm afraid. You must come.'

Ralph paused for a moment. Then he put on his coat and hat and followed Tim Linkinwater.

'What have you got to tell me?' he said to the Cheerybles when he arrived.

'It's about a death,' said brother Charles.

Ralph's eyes brightened for a second. 'Is it my nephew?'

'You should be ashamed of yourself!' said brother Ned. 'You're a hard-hearted, unnatural man. We are here to tell you about the death of a poor, innocent boy – a warm-hearted boy who never knew love, who never did harm to anybody. A boy who has died because of you.'

'Just tell me that my nephew is dead,' Ralph said. 'That's all I want to hear.'

A figure stepped out of the shadows into the centre of the room. It was Brooker. 'These gentlemen are talking about your only son,' he said quietly. Ralph stared in silence as Brooker told his story. 'Twenty-five years ago,' he said, 'you secretly married a girl for her money. You had a son, but you sent him away so that nobody would know about the marriage. Seven years later, your wife ran away with another man. She died soon afterwards. Although your wife was dead, you still wanted revenge.

'That's when you met me. I was a rough, hard-drinking man in those days. I had lost all my money. You wanted me to find your child, and I agreed. I brought the child home to you, but you weren't grateful. You treated me badly, and I began to hate you. I, too, wanted revenge. Eight years ago, while you were away on business, I took your child to a school in Yorkshire – Dotheboys Hall. After your return, I told you that your son had died.

'A short time later, I was sent abroad on a prison ship. When I returned, I went to Dotheboys Hall to find the boy. I heard that he had run away with an assistant schoolteacher – called Nickleby! – so I came to London to find you. I wanted to tell you about your son, hoping that you would give me money for the information, but you refused to listen. I discovered from Newman Noggs that the boy was very ill and had gone to Devon, so I went down there to see him. Unfortunately, he saw me watching him from behind a tree and was frightened. When I returned to the farmhouse a few days later, your nephew told me that the boy was dead. This is my story. I've been a bad man, I know, but I want you to know what you've really done. You tried to punish your nephew, but you killed your own child instead.'

When Brooker finished, there was silence in the room. Suddenly, Ralph Nickleby picked up the lamp and threw it to the floor. In the darkness and confusion, he escaped.

As he ran home, there was an unfamiliar feeling in his heart – pain. He had always been scornful of people who suffered from broken hearts – he had always believed that they were lying. Now he knew what such pain felt like, and it frightened him.

When he reached home, he sat alone in his room with his head in his hands. He had been blinded by his hate for Nicholas, and had murdered his own child! He could not believe it. He had tried to destroy the only person in the world who had shown his son love. What good was all his money now?

He had murdered his own child.

Interrupted by a loud knocking at the door, he opened the window and called down into the street, 'Who is it?'

'The twins want to know what to do with Brooker,' an unknown voice called up from the darkness.

'Tell them to bring him here tomorrow,' Ralph replied. 'Bring my nephew with them.'

'At what time?'

'In the afternoon. It doesn't matter what time.'

Ralph closed the window and returned to his chair. A church bell struck one o'clock. Rain began to fall. The glass in the window shook in the wind.

'My nephew was right,' Ralph said quietly to himself. 'It's the end.'

CHAPTER 14

Happiness at Last

Nicholas's happiness was complete. He was with all the people that he loved. All his enemies had been defeated.

T he same evening, Nicholas returned home from Devon and there was much crying and sadness over poor Smike's death. Then Kate told him everything about his uncle.

The next day, the Cheeryble brothers, Brooker and Nicholas arrived at Ralph Nickleby's house. Although they knocked loudly on the door, there was no answer. Soon, a large group of neighbours were standing outside the house. One man climbed through a window at the back and let everybody in. They searched every room, but there was no sign of Ralph. Finally, they reached a room at the top of the house.

'It's very odd,' one of the neighbours whispered. 'He's hiding in the dark behind the door. Look.'

Everyone pressed forwards to see. Then one of them pushed the others to one side and ran in with a loud cry. He took a knife from his pocket and cut down the body.

Ralph had hanged himself.

◆

After a few weeks, the shock of these events slowly passed into memory. Madeline got better and moved in with the Cheeryble brothers, who treated her like a daughter. Kate was sad to see her friend leave, but Nicholas was relieved. He did not want anyone to know that he was in love with Madeline.

One day, the Cheerybles invited Nicholas, Kate, Mrs Nickleby and Miss La Creevy to dinner. When they arrived, brother Charles took Kate by the arm.

'Have you seen Madeline, my dear,' he said, 'since she left your house?'

'No, sir,' Kate replied. 'Not once. I've only received one letter from her. I expect that she'll soon forget all about me.'

'Well, if you go into that room,' Charles said, 'there's a letter from her for you on the table.'

When Kate had gone, Charles asked Nicholas to follow him into his private room. Nicholas was surprised to see Frank Cheeryble.

'I thought you'd gone abroad again!' Nicholas said.

Charles watched with a big smile while the two young men shook hands. 'I'm glad,' he said. 'I want you two to be good friends.'

He then showed Nicholas a copy of Madeline's grandfather's **will**. Nicholas read until he reached the line: *Madeline Bray will receive a house valued at twelve thousand pounds when she gets married.* He did not know what to say.

Charles turned to Frank. 'My brother and I love Madeline very much. You saved this will from the fire, and we would be very happy if you married this girl. What do you say?'

'No, I can't,' Frank said. 'She's in love with a man who deserves her more than me. I love another woman.'

'Mr Nickleby's sister?' Charles asked with amusement.

While Frank was trying to think of a reply, Charles took Nicholas's hand with a warm smile. 'I know that Madeline loves you, Mr Nickleby, and my brother and I are very happy. We are equally happy with Frank's choice of wife. Would you, sir, allow him to marry your sister?'

At that moment, the door opened and brother Ned came in with Mrs Nickleby, Kate – and Madeline!

'Did you find the letter?' Charles asked, taking Kate's hand. 'Or did you find Madeline herself?'

Everybody started laughing, shaking hands, hugging and kissing each other. Little Miss La Creevy sat in a window-seat and cried with happiness. Tim Linkinwater, who had known Miss La Creevy for a long time, put his arm around her shoulders. When Newman Noggs arrived, Nicholas's happiness was complete. He was with all the people that loved. All his enemies had been **defeat**ed. Dinner that night was probably one of the happiest dinners in history!

Nicholas wanted to share his happiness with everybody, so a few days later he travelled to Yorkshire to see John Browdie and his wife, Tilda. They were excited to see him. Tilda prepared an enormous breakfast and they sat around the table in the warm kitchen, talking. Eventually, the conversation turned to the subject of Squeers.

'They were talking about him in town last night,' John said. 'News from London is very slow to reach us here. They say that he's been sent to prison for seven years. Is that true?'

'Yes. He's been sent abroad on a prison ship for stealing a will.'

John Browdie laughed loudly, hitting the side of his enormous leg with his hand. 'If the news has reached Dotheboys Hall, I wouldn't like to be in the old woman's shoes. Or Fanny's either! Let's go and find out.'

---

will /wɪl/ (n) a legal document that says who should have your money after you die
defeat /dɪˈfiːt/ (n) the end of a game or fight, when someone has lost

But Nicholas refused. 'I'll only make things worse for them both if I go, too,' he said.

'That's true,' John agreed.

He kissed his wife, shook Nicholas's hand and rode through the snow to Dotheboys Hall on his horse.

When he arrived, he heard a loud noise coming from inside the school. The news about Squeers had already reached Dotheboys Hall! The boys had locked Mrs Squeers and Fanny into the classroom and were breaking all the furniture. They had stolen Mrs Squeers's hat and forced her to her knees. One of the boys was pushing a long wooden spoon into her mouth. He was making her take her own 'medicine' – the horrible thick soup that she usually made them eat! Another boy was pushing young Wackford's head into the pot of soup.

When John saw other boys attacking Fanny Squeers, he rushed into the room. 'What's happening here, boys?' he shouted.

'Squeers is in prison, and we're going to run away!' they shouted back. 'We won't stay! We won't stay!'

'Well, don't stay,' John said. 'But don't hurt the women.'

The boys cheered loudly. A few minutes later, the school was empty. All the boys had run away.

'You'll pay for this, John Browdie!' Fanny Squeers said angrily. 'You've helped our boys run away!'

John looked at her quietly for a minute, then said, 'I'm glad your father is in prison, Fanny. He deserves his punishment. But if you need a friend, don't forget Tilda and me. We'll be glad to help you if we can.'

With those words, he hurried back to his wife and Nicholas. For the next few days, the countryside was filled with boys. John and his wife helped as many as they could. They gave them food and money. Some boys were found crying under trees in the snow. One poor child was found dead beside the road, frozen to death. But soon, most of the boys had returned to their families.

Dotheboys Hall became just a dark and painful memory.

◆

Nicholas and Madeline married a few months later. On the same day, Kate Nickleby became Mrs Frank Cheeryble. Then Miss La Creevy married Tim Linkinwater in secret.

Nicholas put the money that he received from Madeline into the Cheeryble brothers' business, which became known as 'Cheeryble and Nickleby'. The brothers stopped working, and were free to enjoy the happiness that they had given everyone else.

Ralph Nickleby had not left a will, but nobody wanted to touch his money, so eventually the government took it all. His money, the most important thing in his life, had made no one happy.

As soon as he became rich, Nicholas bought his father's old house in Devon. As the years passed, he and Madeline had several children. Kate and Frank Cheeryble also had children. They moved into a house not far away, and the two families spent many happy times together. Mrs Nickleby sometimes lived with her son, sometimes with her daughter.

A quiet, grey-haired gentleman lived in a little cottage near Nicholas's house. His main pleasure in life was playing with the children. The children all loved dear old Newman Noggs.

Every spring and summer, by the rose-tree in Nicholas's garden, the children always made sure that there were fresh flowers on Smike's **grave**. Although they had never known him, they spoke about him softly, with tears in their eyes. They knew that he had once been their father's only friend. To them, he would always be their much-loved cousin, Smike.

grave /greɪv/ (n) the place in the ground where a dead body is put

1 Guilty or not guilty?

Imagine that Ralph is still alive.
The judge is deciding whether
Ralph should go to prison or not.
Work with two other students and
have this conversation.

Student A: You work for the government. You think that Ralph should go to prison. Talk about all the bad things that he has done and the people that he has hurt. Explain why he is a danger to society.

Student B: You are speaking for Ralph. You think that Ralph has suffered enough and should not go to prison. You do not believe that he has done anything really criminal. In fact, you believe that we should all feel sorry for him. Try to persuade the judge that Wackford Squeers, Mr Snawley and Sir Mulberry Hawk should go to prison instead of Ralph.

Student C: You are the judge. Ask careful questions. Make the other two people defend their opinions. Then make your final decision about Ralph.

2 Work with other students. Discuss the statements and answer the questions. Do you agree with the statements? Why (not)?

A 'In this story, all the people with power and/or money are bad. All the good people have no money and suffer cruel, unfair treatment.'
Is it more difficult to be a good person if you are poor? Why (not)?

B 'Chance and luck play a very important part in the story.'
How important is luck in real life?
What is the luckiest thing that has ever happened to you?
What is the unluckiest?

1 Write an advertisement for Dotheboys Hall. Make it sound a perfect place to send a child.

DOTHEBOYS HALL
for a perfect start in life!

....

....

....

....

....

....

....

....

2 Imagine that you work for the government as an inspector of schools. After you have visited Dotheboys Hall, you make a list of eight problems with the school and your suggestions for improvements.

	Problems	Suggestions
1		
2		
3		
4		
5		
6		
7		
8		

1 Charles Dickens wrote about the social problems of ordinary people in Britain in the early 1800s. Discuss the pictures below. What problems do they suggest?

In groups, make notes about living and working conditions at that time. Use the pictures opposite and the Internet or books to help you.

....
....
....
....
....
....
....

Schooling   **Housing**   **Health**

Life in Dickens's time

Law and punishment   **Children**   **Family life**

....
....
....
....
....
....

3 Discuss living conditions in your country. What changes have there been since your grandparents were children? Make notes.

	Past	Present
Schooling		
Health		
Law and punishment		
Housing		
Family life		

4 Life for many people is more comfortable today because of the mechanical, electrical and electronic equipment that we can use. List ten pieces of equipment or other inventions that are used every day now but which were not used in your country fifty years ago. Then choose, from your list, the two things that you think have changed life most. Discuss your choices with other students. Try to make them agree with you.

1 .... 6 ....

2 .... 7 ....

3 .... 8 ....

4 .... 9 ....

5 .... 10 ....